Cruising Skipper

John Mellor

Fernhurst Books

First published in 1991 by Fernhurst Books, 33 Grand Parade, Brighton, East Sussex.

Printed and bound in Great Britain.

British Library Cataloguing in Publication Data

    Mellor, John, *1945-*
    Cruising skipper.
    I. Title
    797.125

ISBN 0 906754 71 2

Acknowledgements
The author and publishers would like to thank Rosie Kempner for providing the yacht *Polar Star* for photography, Peter White of the Seafever Sea School for providing and driving the camera boat, and Linda Edmonds, Carolyn Yates and Tim Davison for crewing on camera.

Photographs
All photographs by John Woodward, with the exception of the following:
Andrew Bray: pages 32, 84.
Julia Claxton: pages 19 (top), 21.
John Mellor: pages 9, 11 (bottom), 12 (top), 22 (R), 23, 25, 62, 63, 78, 88, 91 (both).
RFD Ltd: page 26.
Yachting Photographics: cover.

Edited and designed by John Woodward
Composition by Central Southern Typesetters, Eastbourne
Artwork by PanTek, Maidstone
Printed by Ebenezer Baylis & Son, Worcester.

Contents

Introduction

Many people think that a good sailor is synonymous with a good skipper, but they are wrong. The ability to sail well is useful to a skipper, but not essential; adequacy is quite sufficient. What is essential is the ability to command – because it is commanding, not sailing, that constitutes the major role of a cruising skipper.

A vessel at sea cannot be run by committee or consensus, for the simple reason that time or safety rarely permit the luxury of discussion. A ship must be run by one man – or woman – who has the experience, the seamanship skills and the power of command needed to both sail her safely and organise the crew efficiently.

Aboard small yachts in this technological and egalitarian age all too many of us lose sight of the need for this 'power of command'. A skipper is right to improve his seamanship and sailing expertise, but quite wrong to think that he must actually pull on the ropes himself. With sufficient ability to command his crew and delegate the work, a good skipper ought to be able to run his ship while lying in his bunk with a broken leg.

Command and decision-making

As a young officer under training at Dartmouth Royal Naval College many years ago I was told that 'there is no such thing as a bad decision, only a badly-made one'. This is an interesting statement that has far-reaching implications for a cruising skipper, so it bears some analysis.

A badly-made decision is one that is communicated to the crew in a half-hearted manner, then carried through in similar vein. A basically sound decision may be technically incorrect according to the book, but if it is implemented firmly and with conviction it will likely produce a better result than a technically correct one which is not. But do not confuse lack of conviction with the perfectly valid business of altering a plan to suit changing circumstances; decisions must be pursued with determination, but not blindly.

Although it is true that some people are natural, instinctive leaders and others find leadership quite beyond them, the majority of us can make a very reasonable job of it given some guidelines. There is a technique to skippering just as there is in any profession, and it is important to learn it. Skippering is a specific, specialist job, not a role that can be simply filled by the owner, or the most experienced member of the crew. This book is about that job.

PART ONE

THE ROLE OF
THE SKIPPER

1 Assessing the boat

When a cruising skipper stands on the quayside and surveys a boat, the three qualities that he will look for first are ease of handling, directional stability, and her capacity for keeping him safe from harm. Although all three are closely associated with virtually every design characteristic of the boat, we can loosely consider ease of handling to be a function of the rig and directional stability a function of the hull. Assuming these two are suitable for a cruising boat, the capacity for keeping him safe is a function of her fixtures and fittings.

THE RIG

Although it may sound like heresy I shall include the engine under this heading. The reason is simple: the modern marine diesel engine is so reliable, so powerful and so efficient that it can

be regarded as an integral part of the motive power of a cruising yacht; indeed sailing waters are often so congested these days that it *must* be considered so. When we refer to ease of handling as a function of the rig, we really mean that it is a function of the propulsion system generally.

Having said that, let us first look at the rig itself and how it can be made to give easy and reliable handling. The modern combination of roller-reefing genoa and mast-reefing mainsail is, assuming nothing jams, about the easiest rig to handle that one could imagine. Pull one rope and the sail sets; pull another and it reefs; pull further and it stows. The Achilles Heel of this rig, of course, lies in that little phrase 'assuming nothing jams'. The danger with these systems is that if they do go wrong they will almost certainly 'fail-danger' rather than 'fail-safe'. The risks inherent in a large genoa jamming half rolled up in the face of a rising gale are clearly enormous, and you should think very seriously before committing yourself to such a rig. Traditional reefing systems combined with a selection of headsails are more reliable than roller-furling, but they do involve a lot more work, especially for a husband and wife crew.

The different types of sail and rig – ketch, cutter, schooner, gaff, Chinese lug and so on – all have their handling idiosyncracies which need to be considered carefully if you have to sail one of them. Most yachtsmen these days grow up with simple Bermuda-rigged sloops and often have difficulty analysing how anything else works. Basically, balancing the sailplan is a matter of visualising the effect on the Centre of Effort when one sail is removed or reefed. If you think of the Centre of Lateral Resistance of the hull as being roughly halfway along the keel, then adjust your sails to put their combined Centre of Effort roughly just abaft this (to give slight weather helm) you will not go far wrong.

◊ *Roller-furling sails are easy to handle, but what if they jam?*

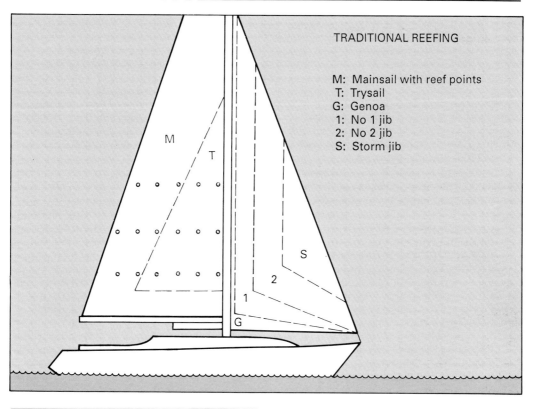

TRADITIONAL REEFING

M: Mainsail with reef points
T: Trysail
G: Genoa
1: No 1 jib
2: No 2 jib
S: Storm jib

⇦ *They may be hard work, but a selection of headsails, slab-reefing main and trysail are still the most dependable option.*

Engine installation

Modern marine diesel engines are so powerful, quiet and vibration-free that there is really no reason for having any other type of auxiliary. A diesel is cheap to run, very simple, extremely reliable, and uses safe fuel that is easily obtainable virtually anywhere in the world. What more could a cruising skipper want from his engine?

Whatever type of engine is fitted, the installation must be accessible for maintenance and repair at sea in bad weather, and the regular maintenance schedule must be adhered to religiously. Most sailing skippers' engine problems stem from simple lack of care and attention to the thing.

◊ *The four-sail rig of this old-fashioned gaff cutter is more complicated than that of a bermudan sloop, but the mix of sails gives more flexibility when reefing or manoeuvring.*

THE SHAPE OF THE HULL

As a cruising skipper, your primary concern here is stability. There are two elements to this: directional stability and lateral stability. The first is a boat's tendency to run in a straight line, and the second is her tendency to stay upright. Both are related to her sea-keeping qualities, and directional stability will also affect her manoeuvring and handling.

The directional stability of a boat can be judged from the shape of her underwater profile. The diagram opposite shows four types of profile that cover the full range of normal boat types. If you imagine each boat turning about its midpoint, as shown, it should be apparent that the top shape will present a lot more resistance to the water than the bottom one. This means it will turn more slowly and be less responsive when manoeuvring, but in open water this apparent disadvantage proves beneficial since the boat's inclination will be to run straight. By contrast the fin and spade configuration is highly manoeuvrable but will tend to turn under the slightest influence – wave under the stern, unsteady hand on the tiller – and so will be considerably less directionally stable. The two shapes between these extremes will behave accordingly.

You will notice that the two upper hull shapes are deeper in the water at the stern. This ensures that if the boat swings off course the extra water pressure on the larger aft profile tends to push her back. As a result the boat runs straight.

In calm water these assessments stand as they are, but at sea the situation is slightly more complex owing to the fact that the hull constantly changes its immersed shape as the boat heels and rolls under the influence of wind and waves. The cross-sectional shapes of the bow and stern (the entry and run) have a considerable influence on directional stability at sea, particularly when running or reaching down waves. In principle the shape of each end affects its buoyancy: a full stern, for example, will lift far more readily to a wave, and with greater force, than a fine one. If the stern lifts, the yacht is likely to swing broadside-on to the wave (broach), and this tendency will be made worse by a fine bow with little buoyancy which can be easily submerged,

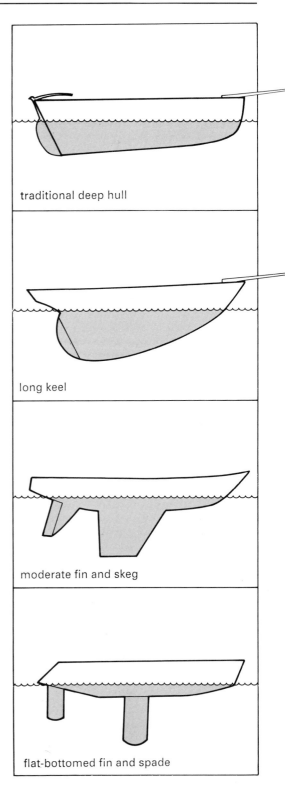

traditional deep hull

long keel

moderate fin and skeg

flat-bottomed fin and spade

providing grip forward for the stern to pivot round. Many modern racing yachts have this unseamanlike hull shape, but a good cruising yacht needs a modicum of buoyancy forward so that the bow will lift to a wave, and not so much aft.

FIXTURES AND FITTINGS

The first requirement here is a proper sea-going layout both on deck and down below, so that the boat can be worked easily and comfortably in all weathers. The priorities down below are cooking, navigating and sleeping; priorities on deck are steering, watchkeeping and sail-changing.

⟁ The difference in handling characteristics between these two keel profiles should be apparent at a glance.

⟁ With her full stern, the yacht on the left could prove a handful in a following sea. The fine stern on the right is more suited to cruising.

Down below this means proper handrails, narrow bunks, seats or straps for the navigator and cook to wedge themselves into, wet oil-skin stowage clear of the main accommodation, plenty of well-ventilated stowage places, some way of drying wet clothes, and somewhere to sit clear of those asleep. It means accommodation that is easily cleaned to avoid squalor in bad weather (especially near the galley). It means proper lee-cloths or deep bunkboards so that you can sleep in the weather bunks as well as the lee ones while underway. It means a chart table that is well protected from the weather, so that the navigator is not constantly being deluged with water. It means proper night-lighting (red is best) so that you can work down below without losing your night vision.

On deck it means shelter for the helmsman and watchkeeper, in the form of a pram hood and spray dodgers, and cockpit seats that drain so that they do not sit for hours in pools of water. It means a compass that is sited and lit for ease of use on either tack at any angle of heel, and a headsail rigged and sheeted to give vision under the lee bow. It means a cockpit that is narrow enough for you to brace your feet on the opposite seat, and deep enough for you to sit comfortably with your feet on the sole. It means a strong eyebolt by the bridge-deck so that you can clip on your harness before leaving the cabin, and jackstays that you can reach from within the cockpit.

A good cruising skipper will go to some trouble to set his boat up in a proper seamanlike manner such as this. He knows that a comfortable, dry and well-organised boat is a safe and efficient one that is a pleasure to sail.

⌂ A good sea-going deck layout. Note the non-slip decking, plenty of space to work around the mast and the simple, secure grabrails. Several control lines have been led aft so they can be worked from the safety of the cockpit.

SEA TRIALS

Although an experienced skipper can learn a great deal about a boat from simply looking (enough in fact to make a perfectly competent job of handling her) it is only by running proper sea trials that he can develop the confidence that will enable him to handle her well in all situations. With this in mind, you should check the characteristics listed below.

Under power
- How quickly she accelerates, from rest and from underway, going ahead and going astern.
- How quickly she stops, from various speeds both ahead and astern, slowing in neutral and using the opposite gear for emergency stop.
- How quickly she turns, both ways, going ahead and in neutral, using just the rudder.
- How sharply she can be turned by kicking ahead in bursts with the rudder over, and also by making a three point turn.
- How she swings due to prop effect, kicking ahead and astern, and how the effect diminishes on getting underway.
- The slowest speed at which she will steer, both ahead and astern, using just the rudder.

Under sail
- The time and sea-room she needs to tack and gybe, and also to stop when luffed head-to-wind.
- Her behaviour when left alone with sheets freed and helm loose.
- Her behaviour when you heave-to with mainsail and backed jib.
- The speed she sails at under bare poles.
- How she sails, tacks and gybes under mainsail alone, and jib alone.
- How quickly you can turn her by backing the jib or hardening the main.
- The slowest speed at which she will reliably tack, in various conditions of wind and sea.

Having checked out all these you should spend some time going round in figures of eight just to get the feel of the boat: tacking, gybing, trimming sails, steering and playing with the throttle under power. Practise stemming a buoy and going alongside it as though it were a pontoon. A few hours of this at the beginning of the season, or on taking over a strange boat, will be time very well spent.

2 Handling the crew

You should now understand the qualities of a good cruising yacht. As a skipper, however, you should no more be thinking of actually sailing this yacht than an Eskimo will think of pulling his sledge. He has a team of huskies to do the job, and you have a crew. If you can handle them well, they will handle the boat.

TRAINING THE CREW

Few amateur yacht skippers can enjoy the luxury of choosing their crews, since most select themselves by virtue of marriage, birth or friendship. However, it is instructive to consider the qualities exhibited by the ideal crew, since you will need to encourage these in the crew you actually have. We can also look at ways of dealing with undesirable qualities so that we can turn unsatisfactory crews into good

ones. Very occasionally one finds an impossible crew, but most bad crews, like bad dogs, seem to belong to bad handlers.

Ask a number of skippers for their most important requirement in a crew and the majority will say experience. Although experience is clearly useful you should appreciate that you can give this to your crew yourself; what you cannot give them is character, and the right sort of this is infinitely more important than any amount of experience. Willingness and reliability are the two most useful qualities that a crew can possess, and it is very much in your interest to encourage them.

Probably the most constructive way of doing this is to make your crew feel individually important, which of course they are. Keep them informed, so they know what is happening

▷ *Keep your crew informed and involved.*

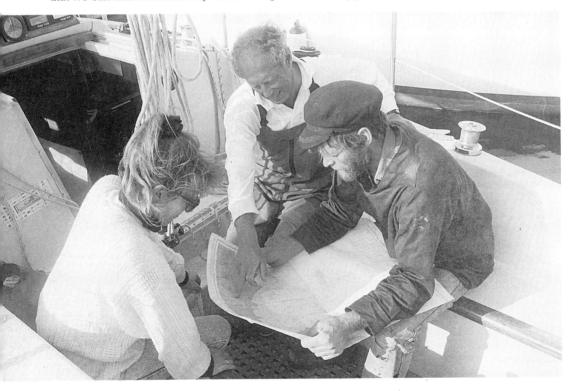

and what is planned. Keep them interested and involved so that they feel a part of it all, so that you and your crew operate as a team pulling together. Praise them loudly in public when they do something well; correct them quietly in private when they do something wrong.

As a skipper you must be, and be seen to be, both fair and firm. It is essential for the safety of the boat that your crew obey you without question when necessary, but if circumstances permit the luxury of discussion, then let them have their say – on destinations, sailing times and so on. Respect for your power of command and your seamanship will make your crew reliable, but it is your consideration for their welfare that generates willingness, and their willingness makes them not only highly efficient crew members but also excellent companions.

You may think that all this sounds rather professional and does not really apply to the skipper cruising with family and friends. Believe me, it is far more difficult to command a crew that knows you well than it is to command professionals who not only do not know you, but have been trained to accept both the skipper's command and his importance. The professional crew will assume that you know what you are doing until you prove to them otherwise; the family crew will be the opposite! Not only must you convince them that you are a capable and competent skipper who is worthy of command, but also that you are not a frustrated 'Cap'n Bligh' who will rant and rave and generally make their lives a misery.

Bear in mind that both you and your crew are sailing for the pleasure of it; if you do not get on with each other you would be well advised to suggest they go and sail with someone else. Try to avoid discovering from bitter experience that a man is so full of his own importance that he completely ignores your instructions when on watch at night and does what he thinks is best. Crews like this are a danger to everyone they sail with and should be left in the garden where they belong.

There is rarely any need for a skipper to shout at his crew. If your crew respect you they will instinctively look to you for guidance and orders, many of which can be arranged before a manoeuvre and simply confirmed by a nod of the head when required. Let us take a closer look at this business of actually giving orders to the crew, as your standing with them may depend on how you do this.

BRIEFING THE CREW

As we will see in Part Two, when we look at handling the boat with the crew, many manoeuvres can (and should) be preplanned, either as laid-down standing routines or immediately before carrying out the manoeuvre. A simple example is when anchoring. Thoroughly brief your crew as to exactly how you propose to approach the anchorage, where you intend letting go the anchor, in what depth of water, and how much cable you will want. You will also need to give full details of how you want the sails handling so that each crew member knows exactly what is going to happen generally, and precisely what will be expected of him personally and when.

↷ *Brief your crew well before a manoeuvre, and it should go like clockwork.*

⌂ Once everyone knows what they are doing, there is no need for shouting and drama.

You could detail one crew member to take soundings with the lead or watch the echosounder while another stands by to let go the anchor. You might tell them both to prepare the anchor for letting go (flaking the cable on deck) during the early stages, and hand the sails as required before moving to their specific posts in readiness for the final approach. Deciding who does what should, of course, be based on their respective abilities. Sounding, for example, is best left to someone whose attention is not easily distracted, while the cable should be flaked and the anchor lifted over the rail by someone reasonably strong. The precise way in which you word your orders will also depend on the crew's experience. One crew member can simply be told to 'set the number one jib', while another may have to be carefully instructed to 'get the green sailbag on deck, pull out the corner of the sail that is at the top of the bag, shackle it to the stemhead . . .'

As you slow down and round up into the tide a well-briefed crew will know what is happening and, most importantly, what is about to happen. There will be no need to scream 'Let go the anchor, quickly, now, someone!' when you arrive on station; if you have told the man holding the anchor to watch you a simple nod of the head will suffice as an order; he knows that letting go the anchor is what you now want him to do, and that twenty metres is the amount of warp you want letting out (because you have already told him). Everyone will be calm; everyone will be ready; and everyone will be impressed, because the manoeuvre will go like clockwork.

MANAGING THE CREW

Besides organising the crew to sail the boat and looking after their welfare on board, the skipper should also be responsible for any facets of the crew's life that may affect the boat or the lives of those aboard her. This means ensuring they get ashore safely, and back aboard again. It means arranging their joining and leaving times and their travelling if they come some distance to sail with you. It also means ensuring they do carry passports and do not carry contraband when sailing to foreign ports.

The simplest deficiency can mar a cruise, even ruin it completely. Make sure you have sufficient crockery and cutlery for all the crew and that you have properly organised the victualling; you must not only ensure that you have sufficient stores for the cruise, but also agree with the crew as to who is expected to pay for, or provide, what. It is most important that everyone knows exactly where they stand. When you invite people to sail with you, give them clear instructions as to what you expect them to bring and what will be provided. Food, drink, foul-weather gear and sleeping bag all come into this category.

A very important aspect of the crew's welfare is their health. On a small yacht the skipper is not only master and manager but also medical officer, so he needs to learn something of the subject. There is not space here for a proper discussion of First Aid techniques and I would strongly recommend that you take a First Aid course at night school, and make certain you have on board a well-stocked Medical Chest. Ask your doctor for advice on the contents of this and put in a good First Aid book specifically written for yacht skippers. This should function not only as a reminder for you, but also as a working reference for someone less experienced (it may be *you* lying unconscious on the cabin sole).

Make sure you know about any medical foibles among your crew, and ensure that they bring their own medication – enough to cover the trip and any delays that might conceivably occur. You should also consider equipping the medicine chest with extra supplies, just in case.

The commonest debility at sea is, of course, sea-sickness, and dealing with this can be a subtle business. There is little doubt that there are strong psychological influences at work here, and overt sympathy rarely helps much. Consideration helps – keeping him out of the galley – but good-natured encouragement is usually the most effective way to pull someone

⌂ *Make sure your crew bring the right gear, or in bad weather they will be cold, wet, miserable and inefficient.*

out of the apathy that seasickness brings on. Keeping a sufferer busy in the fresh air is extremely helpful, steering being a particularly useful occupation. Nibbling a dry biscuit may also help overcome the disinclination to eat which is a sign of approaching sickness.

Interestingly, sufferers are generally fine while horizontal in their bunks, but can be totally incapacitated during the thirty seconds spent upright down below while moving from deck to bunk. So if at all possible make them strip off their deck clothes in the cockpit so they can dive into their bunks as fast as they can. Pills and such are a mixed blessing, especially for newcomers to sailing, as they prevent the takers from discovering whether a few hours or days at sea will cure them, as it very often does. Many people feel better if they actually throw up.

3 Shipboard routines

Much of the work your crew has to do in sailing the boat is repeated many times – cooking, cleaning, watchkeeping and so on – and a well-thought-out series of routines will go a long way towards increasing efficiency.

Shipboard routines can be considered under three headings: domestic, sea-going, and emergency. The first covers cooking, cleaning and maintenance while the second covers sailing the boat and sleeping; these normally tie in together in a Watchkeeping Roster so that everyone gets a balanced share of watchkeeping and domestic chores at suitable times. As skipper you will not be popular if someone is woken up in the middle of his precious sleep and told to peel the potatoes! Emergency routines are rather different, being simply lists of the basic, initial actions to be taken in case of particular emergencies.

DOMESTIC ROUTINES

These are not only surprisingly numerous on a boat, but also surprisingly important. Cleanliness may have little to do with Godliness at sea, but the lack of it can have a considerable effect on morale, as can badly-cooked or badly-timed meals. Efficiently-organised domestic routines are an extremely useful weapon in the skipper's armoury, and you should spare no effort in planning them as carefully as possible.

There are three basic tasks to be performed down below on a regular basis: cooking meals, washing dishes and general cleaning. With sufficient crew you may be able to appoint a full-time cook, but normally the way the domestic tasks are allotted to the crew will depend on the watchkeeping system that you are operating. Certain jobs can simply be allocated to each watch on a daily basis, with the watchkeepers doing the work some time during the day when it best suits them. Cooking and washing up, however, need to be organised closely around the watch changeover times, so that both they and the eating itself intrude as little as possible into the rest periods of the off-watch crew.

If numbers permit, you could try this simple system. One of the watch on deck prepares and cooks the meal to be ready about twenty minutes before changeover time. The new watch can be roused ten minutes before this so they can eat in dry comfort, before taking over the watch clutching hot tea or coffee. The old

	CLEANING BELOW	MAINTENANCE ON DECK	PREPARING VEGETABLES
MONDAY	George	Sarah	John
TUESDAY	John	George	Sarah
WEDNESDAY	Sarah	John	George
THURSDAY	George	Sarah	John
FRIDAY	John	George	Sarah
SATURDAY	Sarah	John	George
SUNDAY	George	Sarah	John

watch can then eat and be in their bunks within half an hour, or sit and relax as the mood takes them. One of the new watch can then wash up. If all this is not possible you will have to work out a system to suit your circumstances, bearing in mind that the rosters need to be structured carefully to ensure a satisfactory rotation of tasks. It is worth your while putting as much thought into this as possible, especially when making long passages, as it will colour every moment of every crewman's life, and have a quite dramatic effect on morale. An example of a roster system is shown below.

⌐ *Off-watch, and time to relax.*

Cooking at sea

The difficulties of cooking at sea are such that the cook should be pampered like a prize bull. If you can manage a full-time cook he should never be expected to wash up or clean below; neither should he be expected to keep watch on deck. He will have quite enough to do organising and preparing the meals, and you, the skipper, can do a great deal to help him.

Discuss everything that happens on deck with the cook, so that he can work his cooking

MONDAY	ON WATCH	STANDBY	COOK	WASH UP
2359 – 0300	John	Sarah		
0300 – 0600 ——BREAKFAST——	Sarah	George	George	Sarah
0600 – 0900	George	John		
0900 – 1200 —— LUNCH ——	John	Sarah	Sarah	John
1200 – 1500	Sarah	George		
1500 – 1800 —— SUPPER ——	George	John	John	George
1800 – 2100	John	Sarah		
2100 – 2359	Sarah	George		

⌕ Cooking at sea is no joke, so do whatever you can to make it easier.

and the feeding of the crew around any manoeuvres that are about to take place. Calling all hands to reef in the middle of a meal is not 'part of the rugged sea-going life', it is plain incompetence on the part of the skipper. So is making the cook prepare a full meal in rough weather when a simple snack would see the crew through to an arrival in harbour two hours later. A hearty meal prepared by the cook in calm conditions can then be eaten and enjoyed by everyone in comfort.

Even when cooking has to be done in difficult conditions the skipper can make life much easier for the cook by giving him warning of impending bad weather, and of localised rough seas approaching (tide-rips etc). He can then plan a suitable menu and carry out the more difficult tasks before the rough conditions arrive.

SEA-GOING ROUTINES

The major sea-going routine is watchkeeping, which is dealt with fully in Part Three. This does tend to govern all other regular routines, although domestic cleaning and sea-going maintenance are largely independent of it. The maintenance of the boat herself tends to be forgotten at sea, since most people consider it a winter job. However, on passage there is often little to do, and you can make good use of the time by carrying out a little simple main-

---

MAINTENANCE CHECKLIST
- Mousing of bottlescrews and shackles
- Chafe on bearing surfaces of shackle and clevis pins
- Free movement of blocks and sheaves
- Chafe on halyards and sheets etc
- Security of split rings and pins
- Clear leads of all warps, halyards, sheets, topping lifts etc
- Fractured strands in rigging wire
- Loose fastenings in mast fittings
- Rough edges that could tear sails

⌕ Make out your own checklist of regular maintenance jobs, and use it.

tenance. Cleaning, greasing, oiling, polishing, tidying, stowing gear and repairing sails can all be carried out quite easily at sea in reasonable weather. When in harbour you should go up the mast and check the rigging for wear or damage, and also run through the checks listed below. Keep a maintenance book by the chart table and tell the crew to note in it any defects they find. Every hour spent on maintenance at sea is one hour less that has to be spent on it in harbour. Think about that.

EMERGENCY ROUTINE: ABANDON SHIP!

- Muster in cockpit
- **Bring:**
  lifejacket
  harness
  foul weather gear
- **Skipper brings:**
  emergency bag
  emergency water
  flares
  portable VHF
  yacht's position

READ LIFERAFT LAUNCH PROCEDURE

EMERGENCY ROUTINES

No two emergency situations at sea are ever remotely similar, so you cannot lay down a definite routine to deal with every problem that may arise. However, you can save a lot of time at the onset of an emergency if a clear and simple routine is available that the watch-keeper can put immediately and automatically into operation while you are being summoned. In any emergency there are certain things that must be done right away, and these can be set in motion while you are rubbing the sleep from your eyes and thinking about how to deal with the problem. Such routines can also act as reminders and checklists for you, the skipper, or even complete guidelines for a watchkeeper in your absence.

You should bear in mind that a simple, easily-remembered and easily-performed routine is likely to be more efficient in practice than a complicated one. Some examples are shown below, but it is important that you draw up your own according to the type of boat, crew and sailing area involved. The specific routines that you decide to adopt should be implanted firmly in the minds of all watch-keepers and helmsmen, an excellent method being to fix the instructions to the back of the heads' door. Instruct your crew to study these and encourage them to run through them in

⌂ Make sure everyone on board knows how to use the radio to call for help.

their minds during those long hours on watch. This way the crew will learn the routines, and may even be thinking about them if an emergency suddenly occurs. Radio procedures such as Distress Calls should be posted next to the radio to which they refer (eg MF or VHF), so that even the youngest crew member can simply work his way through the instructions.

Procedures you should adopt for dealing with specific sorts of emergency are examined in more detail in the Appendix.

EMERGENCY ROUTINE: FIRE!

1 Shout FIRE! FIRE! FIRE!
2 Alert all hands
3 Attack fire with extinguishers (make sure they're the right type)
4 Turn boat to minimise fanning from wind and let smoke blow clear
5 Switch VHF to emergency channel 16

READ EXTINGUISHER INSTRUCTIONS

EMERGENCY ROUTINE: MAN OVERBOARD!

1 Shout MAN OVERBOARD!
2 Release lifebelt and danbuoy
3 Note log reading – or press 'Man Overboard' button on electronic navigator
4 Initiate selected MOB recovery method

LEARN SELECTED MOB RECOVERY PROCEDURE

4 Preparing for sea

Ask any deep-sea sailor the secret of sound, trouble-free voyaging and the answer is always the same: good preparation. Serious trouble at sea rarely strikes from the blue, but is usually the end-product of a sequence of minor problems, each problem building on the one before to create a tower of troubles that finally collapses into a genuine emergency. Many of these minor problems stem from poor preparation, and are easily avoided.

We'll look at this in three parts: making the boat ready, equipping her and briefing the crew. The first involves ensuring that the hull, rig and engine are all fit to undertake the projected voyage. The second deals with the stores and equipment that you will need, while the third part is explaining to your crew the workings of this well-equipped boat that you have put together.

MAKING THE BOAT READY

Making the boat ready involves two quite separate activities. The obvious one is the simple business of ensuring that all parts of the

boat are suitably sound, reliable and efficient for their purpose. Less obvious is the matter of being prepared to deal quickly and calmly with any unexpected problems. The secret of smoothly handling an unexpected problem is, of course, to expect it. When preparing a boat for sea you should think not only of all the things that could go wrong, but also all the things that 'couldn't possibly go wrong'; then prepare your boat so that you can deal with both groups.

Having done all this you must assume that nothing on the boat will work properly anyway, and thoroughly test every item of equipment in every way and on every setting. Once you have done this you should be confident that all your equipment works properly, not simply because it is new or recently overhauled, but because you have actually tested it.

Equipping the boat
There seems to be a neurotic obsession with 'safety equipment' these days, to the detriment of good, plain seamanship; a feeling among too many modern yachtsmen that stocking their boats with expensive gear will save them from all the dangers of the sea.

▽ Fit for sea: a smart, well-equipped and comfortable cruising yacht.

▽ Check and test everything, especially problem areas like this mast repair.

⌂ *Both ship and crew are clearly prepared for a rough passage as this well set-up cruising yacht puts to sea in a brisk breeze.*

In truth, a leaky old wreck with no gear other than a teapot will, in the hands of a competent skipper, be a great deal safer than a badly-skippered brand-new yacht equipped with everything that was ever invented for rescuing a sailor from the results of his own incompetence.

Sound seamanship should be the watchword when you fit out your boat. Select each item of equipment and its stowage place only after thorough consideration of the equipment's precise purpose. Before choosing and positioning fire extinguishers, for example, make a careful assessment of where fires may start, what types of fire they are likely to be, and from where they would be best tackled. Consider the possibility of crew being trapped by a fire, and put extinguishers where they can be used to clear a way to safety. If possible put them close to hatches so they can be reached from the deck if necessary as well as from below. Apply the same thinking to lifebelts, liferafts, harnesses, lifejackets, bilge pumps and so on. The diagram shows suggested places for all these things, with the reasoning behind them.

You should apply the same type of thinking to buying and stowing spare parts and tools.

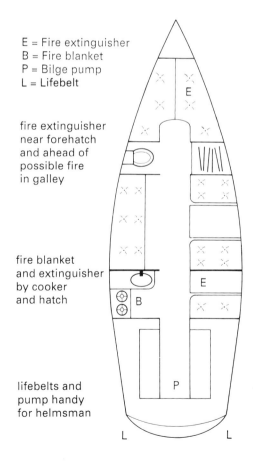

E = Fire extinguisher
B = Fire blanket
P = Bilge pump
L = Lifebelt

fire extinguisher near forehatch and ahead of possible fire in galley

fire blanket and extinguisher by cooker and hatch

lifebelts and pump handy for helmsman

NAVIGATION EQUIPMENT

- Steering compass
- Handbearing compass
- Charts
- Pilot books
- Tidal stream atlases
- Tide tables
- Nautical almanac
- Log book
- Navigator's notebook
- Weather forecast maps
- Echo sounder
- RDF set
- VHF radio

- Long wave radio receiver
- Electronic navigator
- Autopilot
- Log
- Leadline
- Clock
- Barometer
- Binoculars
- Plotter or parallel rules
- Dividers (one-handed)
- Drawing compasses
- Six pencils (2B)
- Soft rubber

Use your common sense when drawing up a list of spares, for it is all too easy (when money permits) to simply purchase two of everything. A great many fittings can be easily bodged while others can be bodged with difficulty, but some cannot be bodged at all and it is these that call for definite spares, perhaps more than one on a long passage if the fitting is essential. Spares for the hard-to-bodge fittings can be carried if space and bank manager permit, while spares for easily-bodged fittings will only clutter up the boat. Make sure you have enough odds and ends of rope, wire, bits of wood, felt and what-have-you for bodging, together with a good array of tools.

Having spare parts on board will do little more than comfort your conscience if you cannot find them when you need them. Apply some rational thought to your stowage, putting things either next to where they might be needed or somewhere logical according to their use. Having done this, draw up a stowage plan and keep it by the chart table for quick reference.

BRIEFING THE CREW

There is no need for everyone in your crew to know everything about the boat – that is the

SEAMANSHIP EQUIPMENT

- Liferaft
- Two lifebelts
- Safety harnesses
- Lifejackets
- Flares
- Foghorn
- Fire extinguishers
- Fire blanket
- Radar reflector
- First aid kit
- Two bilge pumps
- Two torches
- Emergency tiller
- Boarding ladder

- Fenders
- Boathook
- Mooring warps
- Two anchors and warps
- Dinghy
- Two dinghy oars and one spare
- Two crutches and one spare
- Dinghy anchor and warp
- Bailer for dinghy
- Knife and spike kit
- Bucket on lanyard
- Extra warps and lines
- Heaving line

REPAIR EQUIPMENT

- Freeing oil
- Light oil
- Water displacement oil (e.g. WD40)
- Insulating tape
- PTFE tape
- Emery boards and paper
- String
- Gasket cement
- Epoxy rapid glue (e.g. Araldite)
- Resin repair paste (e.g. Isopon)
- Switch cleaner
- Heavy parcel tape
- Wire
- Plastic piping
- General purpose grease
- Tool kit

SPARES

- Batteries
- Bulbs
- Fuses and wire
- Gland packing
- Alternator brushes
- Starter motor brushes
- Distilled water
- Oil for engine, gearbox and reduction gear
- Equipment manuals
- Bilge pump diaphragms
- Bilge pump valves
- All drive belts
- Engine gasket seal
- Fuel, oil and air filters
- Seawater pump impeller
- Foghorn canister
- Stern tube grease
- Hose clips

Petrol engine
- Spark plugs
- Contact breaker points
- Condenser
- Coil
- HT leads
- Distributor cap
- Rotor arm
- Water pump

Diesel engine
- Two injectors
- Set of fuel injection lines
- Water pump impeller

burden you have to carry. You must, however, ensure that each knows enough to fulfil the role you have given him in sailing the boat; that each knows enough to play his proper part in an emergency; and that between them they know enough to get the boat safely home if anything happens to you.

The last possibility is covered in Appendix 1, so let us here consider how they can assist you to rescue the boat in an emergency. The first requirement is that they know exactly where all the essential equipment is and how to use it. Part of this process was discussed in the section on Shipboard Routines, and the rest should be fairly apparent: make sure that the operating instructions for all equipment such as fire extinguishers are clearly visible on or next to the equipment in its normal stowage. Encourage the crew to read these every time they pass.

Make them try any gear that can be used outside of an emergency, such as bilge pumps, harnesses and lifejackets. Fit a harness and lifejacket to each crew member and make him keep them by his bunk so that in an emergency he knows where they are, and that they will fit. Instructions for the liferaft, lifebelts and flares should be pinned by the chart table so that they can be read through regularly by all the crew. If possible, arrange for them to attend a flare and liferaft demonstration (yacht clubs often arrange these for members); there is

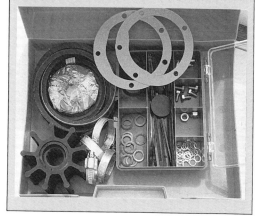

LAUNCHING THE LIFERAFT

Pitch the valise or container overboard and pull on the painter line.

This activates the CO$_2$ gas cylinder which starts to inflate the liferaft.

The gas inflates the buoyancy chambers, boarding step and canopy support.

The inflated liferaft is weatherproof, highly visible, stable and tough.

nothing quite so useful as actually operating a flare, or watching the complete process of launching a liferaft. In a real emergency you will not want them hunting for a torch so they can read the small print on the side of a flare in the dark!

Naturally not all your briefing will be concerned with emergencies – in fact most of it should deal with preventing them occurring in the first place, by the simple expedient of familiarising your crew with the boat herself and the way you skipper her. Show them how the sails operate, reef and stow; how to rig storm sails; how to start the engine and the way the boat behaves under power. Demonstrate the anchoring gear and techniques; show them the mooring warps and fenders, and explain your normal routines when manoeuvring so that they know what you are likely to expect of them. You should actually practise these things, not simply explain them, so that you become confident that your crew can carry them out efficiently. It is particularly important to practise reefing and the rigging of storm sails, both in harbour and at sea; then the crew will be confident of doing the job for real, and you will know that the gear will work properly.

Thorough preparation and equipping of the boat followed by an equally thorough briefing of the crew is a good deal more than half the battle. With that under your belt the rest is almost easy.

▷ *Check your flares – and how to use them.*

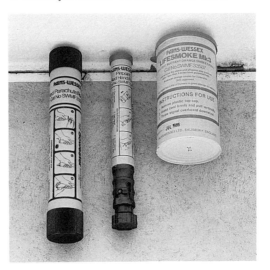

STOWAGE PLAN

A: FOREPEAK
Sea anchor
Drogue
Kedge anchor and warp

B: STARBOARD FO'C'SLE BERTH
Spare sleeping bags and pillows
Towels, cloths

C: PORT FO'C'SLE BERTH
Engine spares
Electrical spares and multimeter
Hand bilge-pump spares

D: FOR'ARD DINETTE SEAT
Canned meats, main meals etc
Tools

E: AFTER DINETTE SEAT
Canned fruit etc

F: HEADS
First aid kit

G: PORT COCKPIT LOCKER
Fenders and mooring warps
Spare dinghy crutches and oars
Boarding ladder
Spare tiller

H: STARBOARD COCKPIT LOCKER
Jibsheets, leadline, heaving line
Buckets and scrubbers
Fishing lines

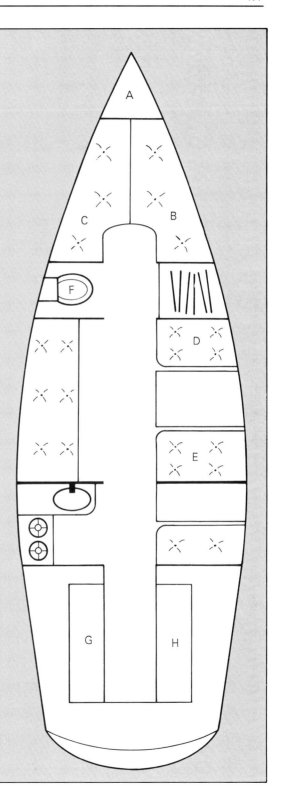

5 Forecasting the weather

Probably the simplest way of ensuring a successful cruise is to get the weather right; it is amazing how well both crew and boat tend to behave when the weather is favourable. It should not be difficult for a day skipper to foresee the pattern over a twelve-hour period, but a cruising skipper needs considerably more skill to predict it for maybe a week ahead, and he must do this if he is to make the best of limited cruising time.

SOURCES OF INFORMATION

There are many different weather forecasts available to a skipper these days – but none of them are infallible, and none of them should be accepted verbatim. The best way to get a reliable picture of the prevailing weather pattern is to note them all regularly over a period of days and draw up a sequence of simple weather charts incorporating all the different forecasts. The forecasts should agree on the positions of current weather features (lows, troughs, fronts etc), but will probably differ in their assessments of speed and direction of movement, as well as any development in terms of deepening, occluding and so on.

This behaviour of weather features is most difficult to forecast, and it is here that we must look for evidence of unreliability.

WEATHER PATTERNS

A skipper's weather forecasting success depends entirely on his ability to assess the changing pattern of the weather that is affecting him. Although assessments are made by the various authorities when they produce forecasts, these are based on information that even in our computerised days is relatively old. They are also based on the meteorologist's judgement of how the weather systems will behave during a fairly long period ahead. Meteorology is not an exact science and it is unreasonable to expect a weather man to make much more than an informed guesstimate as to how the weather will behave at some time in the future. You should understand this and use your own judgement, based on what is happening around your boat, to modify that of the meteorologist. The end result can be surprisingly accurate.

↪ *Keeping track of the weather pattern will help you make your own forecast.*

SOURCES OF WEATHER INFORMATION

- National radio shipping forecasts
- National radio inshore forecasts
- Local radio stations in sailing areas
- Television weather charts
- Newspaper weather charts
- Telephone services (e.g. Marinecall)
- Local coastguard (contact by telephone for current weather conditions at sea)
- Coast radio station forecasts
- National or local weather centre
- Weatherfax machine (synoptic chart)
- Navtex machine (shipping forecast)

In order to assess how the weather pattern is developing you need to understand the actual physical effects of all the wavy lines covering a weather chart. If you know what a cold front looks like in the sky then you can spot when it appears over the horizon – and if you know its speed of advance you can calculate when it will pass over you and produce its characteristic and perhaps important change of weather conditions. There are a great many signs that can help you judge the developing weather, and the interpretation of these signs is known as 'single observer forecasting'.

SINGLE OBSERVER FORECASTING

There are two basic tools that you can use to assess the current weather when you are at sea. One is your eye and the other is the barometer. Your eye clearly goes where you go, but the barometer I have heard described as being 'useful' to have on board. A barometer is ESSENTIAL to have on board, as it can tell you so much about the current weather, the expected future weather and when that future weather is likely to arrive. It probably contributes more to good seamanship and skippering than any other single tool on the boat.

Your first line of attack when judging the weather is to record every single shipping forecast in its entirety. Note each one on a separate sheet (using a printed 'Metmap' form or similar) so that you can compare a number of them in sequence to see the movements and trends of the various systems. Look at the station reports of the actual weather at a number of places to see how far the weather has *actually* progressed compared with how far it *should* have progressed according to the forecast. You should then find it a relatively simple matter to roughly calculate when a particular type of weather will reach you, and make your navigational decisions accordingly. You can then compare this assessment with the features that you observe around you – and the reading and behaviour of the barometer – to polish your predictions to a high degree of accuracy.

The main indicators of weather change are the wind strength and direction, and the cloud formations. A logbook laid out like the one below enables you to keep hourly records of these things so that changes will be noticed as soon as possible. (This is a specimen page from the *Log Book for Cruising under Sail*, devised by the author and published by Fernhurst Books.) You must keep a regular check on these readings as noted by your watchkeepers, and you must stress to them the necessity for accurate records. The amount of cloud cover and the type of cloud, in conjunction with a series of barometer readings and the changing wind pattern, will give a very good indication of the approach of a depression, the impending arrival of a secondary depression, or even an unexpected alteration in the course and speed of a forecast depression.

DATE FRIDAY 14 JUNE 92	FROM DENHAVEN	TO PINTLE CREEK	BUT AT OXLEY MARINA

TIME GMT	COURSE ORDERED	LOG READING (°C)	ESTIMATED COURSE STEERED	DIST RUN	LEEWAY	WIND	SEA	WEATHER	Vis	Bar	POSITION	SOURCE OF FIX	NEXT WP	REMARKS — REFUEL 39 gals ENG HOURS 118·9
														Delivery to Pintle Creek (under power)
														Skipper John Wilson / Mate Rosalie Wilson
0740	⚓	–	–	–	–	NW3	Calm	0/8	G	15	Denhaven Hr	Vis	1	Start engine. Slip. Co & Sp to clear Hr
0805	Var	0	Var	0	–						WP1	RN	4	a/c 240 Set log 0. Set 1500 rpm. Sp 5 kts
0830	240	1.2	240	1.2	nil					15·5	Beach Bn +1 1'	vis		
0855		2.5					slight				½' ↦ Griddle Pier	vis		a/c 250
1000	250	6.5	250			NW4	mod				54°11.5 N·01°13.7 E	RN		
1115		12.0								15	WP4	RN	7	a/c 185
1230	185	18.1	185							14	190° Cresswell Bn 3'	RR		fix NN
1400		25.6						⅛ ♯		13	53°55.1 N·01°07.4 E	RN		
1510		30.2				WS				11	WP7	RN	8	a/c 230
1630	230	35.1	230			S 5/6	m/r	5/8 m	m	09	53°50.0 N·01°02.6 E	RN		Weather and barometer indicate depression – not forecast. Suspect secondary, and severe gales tonight. Will divert to Oxley Marina from WP8
1740		39.4				S 6/7		3/8 L cut		04	WP8	RN	9	a/c 180
1910	180	47.6	180				mod			99	Bell Pt DIP 210	CB		D 9.5
2010		52.2					slight	¼/2 L m R		95	WP9	vis	10	Enter Oxley Creek
2030	⚓	54.3				S 3/4 nil				93	Oxley Marina	vis	–	Enter marina + berth. Stop engine. Refuel

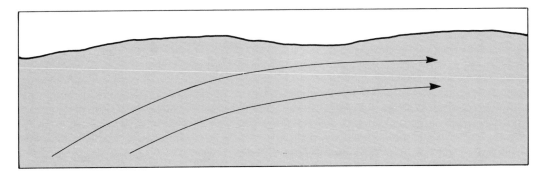

An onshore wind will often show a pronounced bend near the coast.

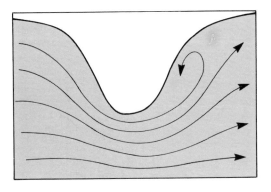

A headland may deflect the wind and set up swirls and eddies.

Steep-sided valleys often act as funnels for violent, localised winds.

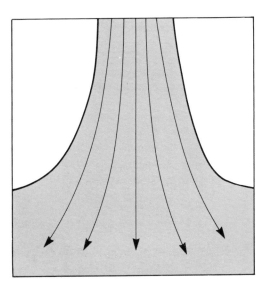

LOCAL WEATHER VARIATIONS

Local geographical features can often have a considerable influence on the forecast weather, and it is particularly important that you are aware of these effects as they will not be predicted by any authority. Most such variations are both minor and very local, but some are capable of transforming a pleasant day's sail into a struggle for survival. Some examples are shown here, but the important thing is to think clearly and rationally about how the weather and sea conditions might be affected by the local circumstances.

Probably the two commonest effects you will experience are the rougher seas caused by the tide running against the wind and the often near-gale conditions caused by a strong sea breeze building up on top of an existing onshore wind. You should also watch out for an increase in strength of perhaps two forces on the Beaufort Scale when a fresh wind blows obliquely onto a coastline. Any one of these effects can make a complete nonsense of the weather forecast, so watch out for them.

POOR VISIBILITY

Even with modern electronic navigators and radar this is still the skipper's nightmare. Careful study of the weather situation can help a great deal by indicating the type of fog you are in, or can expect, and also its direction of approach. You can then either sail clear of the fog if it is localised, or sail clear of the shipping if it is not. Radiation fog, for example, forms onshore and rolls down estuaries into the open sea, rarely extending more than five miles or so offshore. Sea fog, on the other hand, can

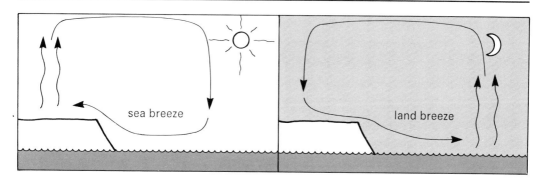

survive a gale of wind and can pop up any-where, especially where strong tidal streams swirl cold water to the surface. A wise skipper will take very different action when faced with these two types.

Radiation fog occurs after hot summer days when clear skies allow the land to cool suffi-ciently at night for the air temperature to fall below its dew point. Fog forms in the colder valleys, close to the ground, and tends to roll down into estuaries and out to sea. Next day the heat of the sun soon 'burns it up' by raising the air temperature above its dew point again, so you will avoid it by waiting until late morn-ing. Otherwise, simply sail further offshore.

Sea fog is commonest in the spring in northern latitudes, when warm, moist south-westerly winds blow over seawater that is still cold from winter. The air is cooled below its dew point and fog forms. It will only be dis-persed by a complete change of weather con-ditions, so the best place to be is in harbour, although a shallow bottom and slack tides may enable the water to warm up and disperse the fog if there is sunshine.

⌂ *Air rising over land by day, and falling by night, creates the sea and land breeze.*

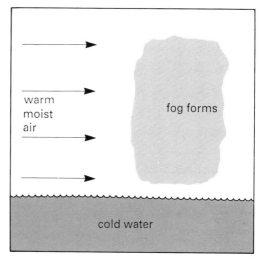

⌂ *Sea fog occurs where the moisture in warm air condenses on contact with cold water.*

⌂ *Radiation fog can often flow out to sea.*

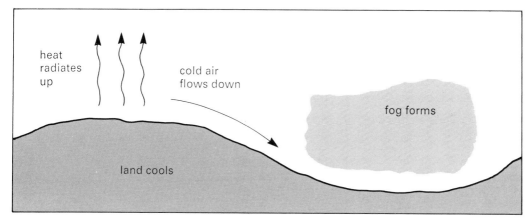

TO SAIL OR NOT

Of the many weather-related decisions required of a skipper, this is possibly the most difficult. The reason, of course, is that when you are faced with the decision you are snug in harbour, and a long way removed from the weather out at sea. In an attempt to resolve this problem many skippers make a virtue of 'going out for a look', but this is not a technique that I personally like. To get out there you must traverse the most dangerous waters of all – shallow inshore waters, often with strong tides and probably offering very little space for manoeuvring. If you get into this lot and discover that the weather is more than you can handle, you are faced with returning to your mooring in the sort of conditions that you probably would not approach the harbour in if you had been at sea. Re-entering harbour in rough weather is always harder than leaving, so the moral is obvious: if in doubt, stay put. One

exception to this thinking is a sheltered weather shore, which enables you to creep out into the rough stuff for a look, retiring from it gracefully and gradually if you do not like what you find.

Generally, a better way is to telephone the local coastguard and ask for a report on the actual weather he is experiencing. He will give you the wind strength and direction and also the sea state, which is usually the major concern. He will also tell you the visibility, which is something you do not want to 'go out for a look at' if there is any chance of it being bad. Check his position on the chart and assess how his weather is likely to affect your proposed passage (which may be in more sheltered, or more exposed waters). Consider describing your boat, crew and intended passage and ask his advice. Remember that your crew must have total faith that you will go to sea only when conditions are suitable. Get this wrong just once and you may well find them busy in the garden next time you want to go sailing.

⇨ *It's better to be in here wishing you were out there, than out there wishing you were in here . . .*

PART TWO

HANDLING
THE BOAT

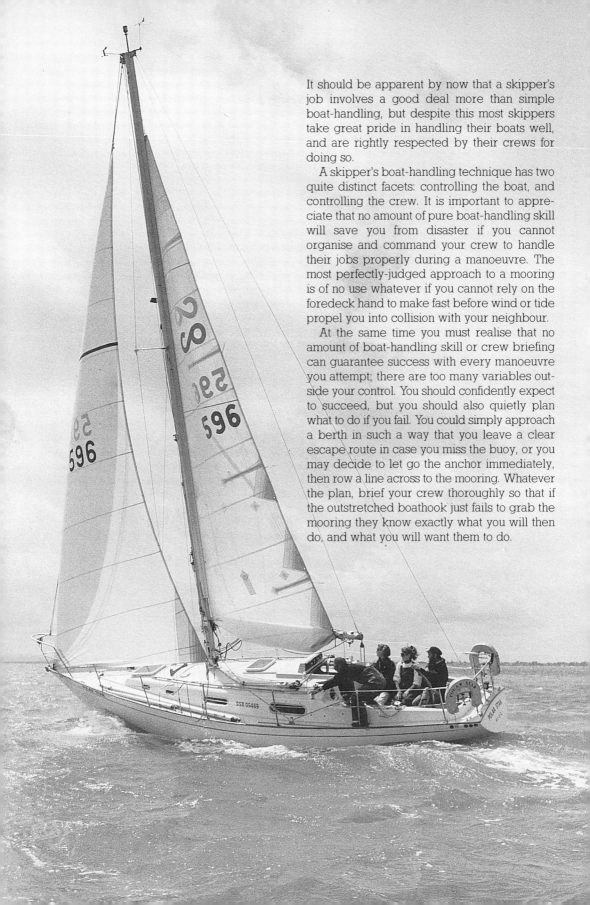

It should be apparent by now that a skipper's job involves a good deal more than simple boat-handling, but despite this most skippers take great pride in handling their boats well, and are rightly respected by their crews for doing so.

A skipper's boat-handling technique has two quite distinct facets: controlling the boat, and controlling the crew. It is important to appreciate that no amount of pure boat-handling skill will save you from disaster if you cannot organise and command your crew to handle their jobs properly during a manoeuvre. The most perfectly-judged approach to a mooring is of no use whatever if you cannot rely on the foredeck hand to make fast before wind or tide propel you into collision with your neighbour.

At the same time you must realise that no amount of boat-handling skill or crew briefing can guarantee success with every manoeuvre you attempt; there are too many variables outside your control. You should confidently expect to succeed, but you should also quietly plan what to do if you fail. You could simply approach a berth in such a way that you leave a clear escape route in case you miss the buoy, or you may decide to let go the anchor immediately, then row a line across to the mooring. Whatever the plan, brief your crew thoroughly so that if the outstretched boathook just fails to grab the mooring they know exactly what you will then do, and what you will want them to do.

6 Handling under sail

There is no intrinsic difference between handling a 90-foot schooner under sail and handling her 12-foot lugsail tender. The main practical difference, of course, is that the single small sail on the dinghy can be controlled easily by one man, but the proliferation of large, heavy sails and complex running rigging found on the schooner requires a small army of men to handle it. This army, if it is to function efficiently, must be controlled by one competent skipper – whose role is not to do things but to organise others to do them.

As skipper, you must be able to stand well back from the operation – both actually and mentally – so you can keep a clear overall view of what is happening. This means that you must be able to trust your crew to get on with the job without having to constantly peer over their shoulders. In principle you should brief them thoroughly on what you want doing, then leave them to it.

↔ *Once your crew know what to do, stand back and let them get on with it.*

Naturally many sail-handling operations are straightforward enough to be managed by a simple prearranged system. This will save a great deal of time and confusion when, for example, all hands are called on deck to put two reefs in the main on a wild night. All the basic handling manoeuvres – setting, handing, reefing and changing sails, tacking and gybing – should have routines worked out and laid down, so the skipper has only to order a particular job done and automatically the right people will pull the right bits of string at the right moment.

This is, of course, only theory. In practice, it probably will not happen like this, so it is absolutely essential that even the most carefully worked-out routine is treated as no more than a skeleton which is fleshed out by the crew member doing the job. All routines should be put together on the assumption that they will go wrong, and they should make specific provision for the most likely snags, such as riding turns fouling up winches when you are short-tacking in a confined space.

⌂ *Mainsail hoist: motor slowly into the wind, set up the topping lift, slacken the sheet and haul away on the halyard.*

SETTING AND HANDING SAILS

These operations may seem too simple to merit organised routines, but in tight spots or windy weather you can get into an awful lot of trouble if things are not done properly and in the correct order. Lowering the mainsail rapidly without taking up on the topping lift, for example, could initiate a sequence of minor calamities that could lead to a real disaster.

You must work out the routines and teach them to the crew, so that when you call for a sail to be handed or set in a hurry you know it will be done instantly and efficiently.

TACKING AND GYBING ROUTINES

Much of the time at sea there is no great hurry for these manoeuvres, so it could be argued that routines are not essential. But things are very different when you are manoeuvring in harbour, especially in any strength of wind, and a clearly-understood routine will go a

⌂ *Tacking: one crew takes the leeward sheet, the other takes the windward.*

The skipper checks the way is clear to windward while the leeward crew prepares to release his sheet.

Helm down, and the leeward crew throws his sheet off the winch...

⌂ The crew in position to tack, with one on each jibsheet winch and the skipper on the helm.

◊ A quiet word, and round she goes. No problem.

long way towards preventing trouble. If necessary you should be able to throw the boat round on a tack or gybe and have the crew automatically follow you without needing the usual warning. You should certainly have routines worked out for dealing with likely problems such as riding turns on the jibsheet winches so that they can be cleared quickly without losing control of the boat.

... then helps haul in the new sheet as the boat turns through the wind.

A last heave on the jibsheet sets the sail properly before it fills with wind on the new tack.

A little opposite helm steadies her on her course while the crew tidy up.

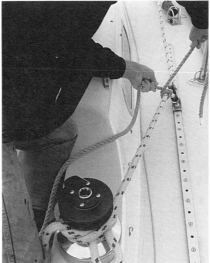

↷ *You can free a riding turn on a sheet winch by tying a second rope to the sheet – using a rolling hitch – and taking it to a second winch. Winding this in relieves the strain, allowing the sheet winch to be sorted out, reloaded and re-tensioned. You can then remove the relief rope.*

Avoid using overlapping genoas when beating in and out of harbour, partly because they tend to sweep the deck, dangerously reducing visibility, and partly because of the risk of them snagging on the shrouds or mast when tacking. Change down to a high-cut Yankee-type jib, or take a suitable number of rolls in a roller-reefing genoa.

REEFING AND CHANGING SAILS

Reefing is likely to be carried out in strong winds and heavy seas, when the noise makes it quite impractical for the skipper to shout instructions from the cockpit, so carefully pre-arranged and practised routines are invaluable. This applies especially to trysails and storm jibs, which often have special sheeting

↷ *Gybing: the skipper holds the old jibsheet while one crew prepares to wind in the new one.*

As the boat bears away the other crew hauls the boom across using the mainsheet.

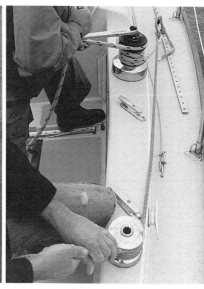

gear. Have your crew rig them in the peace of the harbour so that when they are needed in earnest you know they will work, and the crew will know what to do with them.

When you are cruising there is no need to maintain full speed while reefing or changing sails. Heaving-to will make the boat much safer and more comfortable for reefing, while running off dead before the wind to blanket the headsail behind the mainsail will make the foredeck dry and steady in all but the most violent of seas. This makes a huge difference to crew comfort, dryness, safety and morale.

The boom swings over, the skipper throws the old sheet off the winch and the crew hauls in the new.

HEAVING-TO

This is a most underrated tactic, useful for far more purposes than simply riding out moderately bad weather. It is easy to do, and provides a comfortable and stable platform that can be left to its own devices. While hove-to you can reef, make repairs, stand off to survey an anchorage, or simply have a quiet lunch. However, the efficiency with which a yacht will heave-to depends very much on her directional stability, and some modern short-keel yachts can be most uncooperative.

With the boom squared away the mainsheet is cleated and the jib trimmed to suit.

In essence heaving-to consists of sheeting a headsail to weather and lashing the tiller to leeward. The backed headsail causes the boat to swing downwind whereupon a combination of drive from the mainsail and water flow over the rudder pushes her back again. Within minutes a well-designed boat will settle down with the wind broad on the bow and lie quietly on a fairly steady heading, making minimal way through the water. With full sail set you will probably have to slacken the mainsheet right off to balance the boat. Storm sails should be of such a size that the boat will balance with them sheeted in hard, otherwise the mainsail (or trysail) will flog itself to shreds.

⟳ Reefing while hove-to: free the mainsheet, set up the topping lift and ease the main halyard.

⟳ The easiest way to heave-to is to tack without releasing the old jibsheet. The boat spins around fast owing to the backed jib, but putting the helm hard down counteracts this and holds her steady.

There are various other methods of heaving-to commonly employed for riding out bad weather, but this one is the most versatile for general purposes. The simplest way to achieve it is to tack without freeing the jibsheet so the boat comes round on the new tack already hove-to. This method is useful to bear in mind for emergencies, when you want to stop in such a way that the boat will look after herself. You can sail on again without having to tend the

Pull down the luff and slip the reef cringle over the reefing hook at the gooseneck.

⌂ The classic hove-to position, with the mainsail right out, the jib backed and the tiller held to leeward. Simply lashing the tiller to the nearby winch completes the job.

jib by simply gybing round, although you may have to slacken off the mainsail to allow her bow to pay off.

This method of heaving-to does illustrate rather well how your sails can be used to manoeuvre the boat as well as propel her. Essentially the jib always turns the bow downwind while the mainsail always turns it upwind, the boat pivoting around the rough position of the mast. Understanding this will help you when

manoeuvring in tight spots. If you need to make the boat turn downwind in a hurry, let out the mainsail and/or heave in the jib – or even back the jib. To luff up quickly harden in the main and slacken off the jib; it is usually best not to let it flap completely.

TRIMMING SAILS

Readers who are used to racing will be familiar with the constant tweaking and adjusting of sheets that is required to keep a boat sailing at her best speed. The trimming of sails when cruising is a rather different business – more a

Haul on the reef pendant to draw down the clew, and winch the halyard tight again.

Cleat the reef pendant and halyard. There is often no need to tie up the bunt of the sail.

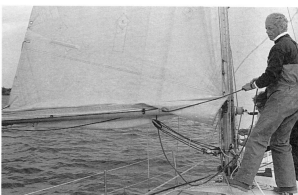

⟳ *Trim the sails, cleat the sheets and relax.*
You're cruising, not racing.

matter of 'nail them down and put the kettle on'. Cruising crews have neither the time nor the inclination to twiddle with the sheets all day long, so the accepted method of trimming is to haul the sheets in a little too much, so that slight variations in the steering or the wind will not cause the sails to flap. But do not overdo this or speed will suffer, the boat will heel excessively and extra strain will be put on the gear.

Although you will normally want to trim the sails to make the boat go as fast as possible, there will be times, particularly in confined spaces such as harbours and rivers, when you will need to sail slowly. You may be approaching a mooring buoy or anchorage, slowing for a

right-of-way vessel to pass ahead of you, allowing your own boat to drift sideways on the tide to get through a gap, or simply intending to take a long look at something before you get too close.

To achieve this all you need do is trim your sails badly; the more inefficiently they are trimmed, the slower you will sail. Do this by either over-sheeting or under-sheeting; of the two, undersheeting is more versatile as the wind can be eventually spilled completely, and the boat will stop. You must remember when doing this that the more slowly the boat is sailing the more slowly she will answer the helm and accelerate when you do trim the sails properly. She will also make a lot of leeway while gathering speed, all of which needs to be borne in mind when sailing in confined spaces. If you want to stop or slow down for any length of time it is better to heave-to than let the sails flog. By adjusting the positions of mainsail and backed jib you can control the speed quite effectively.

It is best to sail on a close reach when you are approaching something that you need to stop by, such as a buoy or man overboard. On this point of sailing you can control the speed of the boat easily by trimming the sails as described above, and sail closer to, or further off the wind to alter your direction of approach. On arrival you can allow all the sails to flap when the boat has stopped, and she will remain stopped. It is wise to hold the boat in a close reach position as you come to a halt rather than luffing up; if she stops with her head to wind you will be unable to control her speed and heading should you need some slight last-minute adjustment.

MAN OVERBOARD RECOVERY

The ramifications of man overboard recovery are discussed in detail in the Appendix, so let us look simply at the accepted methods for returning under sail to someone in the water.

A tried and tested technique is shown opposite. This involves putting the boat onto a reach, tacking, then reaching back along the reciprocal course until you see the casualty. Its great advantage is that in virtually all circumstances it can be inititated by the least experi-

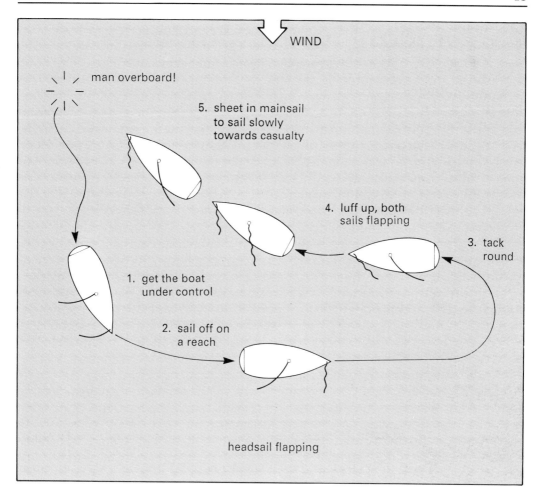

WIND

man overboard!

5. sheet in mainsail
   to sail slowly
   towards casualty

4. luff up, both
   sails flapping

3. tack
   round

1. get the boat
   under control

2. sail off on
   a reach

headsail flapping

enced crewman, and carried through by anyone with the most basic understanding of how to sail. It requires no risky manoeuvring such as gybing, it cannot put the boat in irons with all the attendant dangers of that situation, and it demands no complex assessment of the situation from the helmsman; whatever the point of sailing he simply turns onto a beam reach and carries out the emergency routine that you should have already laid down (see page 21).

A second method in effect abandons sailing and relies on the engine. I find the philosophy behind this rather disturbing as it smacks of panic, but you may find circumstances under which it has merits – if the only person left on board cannot sail competently, for example. Despite this you must be acutely aware of the risks that will be generated by all the rushed

⌂ Man overboard! Reach off, tack, return and approach on a close reach under perfect control. You should be able to point the boat at the casualty with the main and headsail flapping to ensure you can slow down when you come within reach. Get your crew to practise this – it might be you in the water!

activity, the ropes over the side, motoring with the mainsail up, the whirring propeller and so on. It may be better to spend more time teaching your crew to sail.

It may be worth considering a combination of the two methods: you could start the engine on the reach back in case a small nudge of power will rescue a badly-judged approach. However, read the discussion in the Appendix, and the man overboard section in the next chapter.

7 Handling under power

From a skipper's viewpoint this is very much simpler than handling the yacht under sail, since you do not have to organise the crew to handle a complex mass of equipment. It does, however, have its own challenges.

There are two aspects to this topic: *how* to handle a sailing boat under power, and *when* to handle a sailing boat under power. The former is a simple question of boathandling, but the latter needs to be given very careful thought. So let us consider this first.

WHEN TO USE YOUR ENGINE

There is a tendency these days to assume that the engine automatically gives you greater control over a boat than her sails. Certainly there are many occasions on which it will – particularly when there is no wind – but a good skipper will not view his engine as some sort of universal panacea, to be switched on whenever things get difficult.

There are two common situations in which many skippers reach instinctively for the ignition key, without pausing to ponder on whether an engine really is the best solution to the problem. The first is when manoeuvring in a confined space, and the second is when struggling to windward in a rough sea and strong wind.

The danger with the first attitude is that you never learn how to sail the boat, so if you ever need to manoeuvre without an engine you will almost certainly get yourself into trouble. To prepare for this you should take every opportunity to manoeuvre under sail to sharpen up your abilities, keeping the engine ticking over in neutral in case of bother. Very often you will only need a small nudge with the engine to help out a slightly mistimed manoeuvre. Some may consider this cheating, but I call it good seamanship.

The danger of turning to the engine in bad weather is that in these conditions a sailing boat is usually faster, more comfortable, and more efficient under sail than she is under power. A boat under sail automatically negotiates waves at an easier and more efficient angle than a boat under power, and the sails provide considerable stability against rolling. So you should develop the confidence in both yourself and your boat to snug down the sail area to a sensible size and keep her sailing hard.

Motor-sailing is very different from motoring, for it can be a highly effective way of increasing speed under sail, involving very little intrusion from the engine and very low fuel consumption. It is especially valuable when beating to windward in a blow and rough seas. The secret is to sail the boat as though the engine was not running; a few revs will increase speed very noticeably. This technique can also be used in a light breeze with a slop left over from an earlier strong wind; it will keep the boat very much more comfortable than she would be under either sail or power alone. Experiment with the revs.

BASIC HANDLING

There are two secrets to good boat-handling under power: understanding the basic handling characteristics of your boat, engine and propeller – and good, old-fashioned practice. This is where sea trials (see page 13) prove their worth.

In general the handling of a boat under power will depend on the power available, the type of propeller, and the shape of the hull. The windage of the rig and superstructure will also have an influence in strong winds.

A major influence on handling is the effect of the propeller's rotation. As the propeller turns it tends to paddle the stern across in the direction of rotation; the effect is most marked on first engaging gear, and generally more noticeable when going astern than when going ahead. Its strength varies a great deal between boats and installations, and you must check the precise effect by trial. On the face of it prop effect

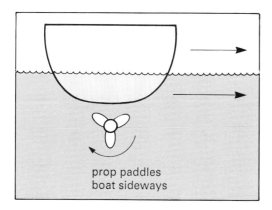

△ Prop effect is inevitable on any single-screw boat. The trick is to use it to your advantage.

is bad news, but it can be extremely useful in the right circumstances as it enables you to swing the stern sideways. When you do not want this to happen you must minimise the effect by increasing speed slowly, or counteract it by swinging the rudder the opposite way before applying the power.

Prop effect is not the only thing to make a boat go sideways when under power. A boat does not have wheels, and the stern does not follow the bow when it turns. Instead, the whole boat slides sideways through the water, at the same time pivoting about a point one-third of the way aft of the bow (roughly by the mast).

▽ The hull's pivot point is roughly one-third back from the bow when you are going forward.

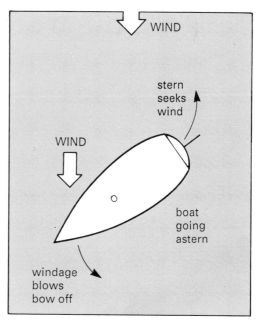

△ As you go astern, windage on the bow will tend to make the stern turn up into the wind.

When you go astern this pivot point moves to one-third of the way forward of the stern. Strong winds will make a boat go sideways to leeward, usually blowing off at the bow first owing to the windage of the mast and rigging; a rolled-up genoa will increase the windage. This tendency, together with the movement aft of the pivot point, causes the stern to turn up into the wind when you go astern in a breeze.

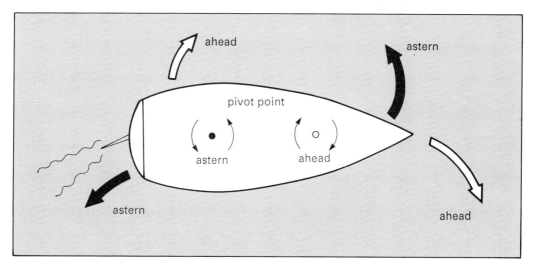

Once you know how your boat handles under power you must decide how best to use it. Modern auxiliary installations generally have considerable reserves of power, yet surprisingly few skippers have the courage to use their engines properly and fully when manoeuvring. You can achieve very powerful turning effects, especially into the wind, by using short bursts of power with the rudder over to kick the stern across. Remember that the turning effect comes from the wash passing across the rudder and being deflected by it, so make sure the rudder is in the right position *before* applying the power. This technique is particularly useful for correcting the attitude of the boat when approaching a berth. A very short,

⌂ The classic three-point turn in a tight corner. With the tiller hard over, kick the boat ahead into the space. As she swings around, go hard astern. Don't bother to change the position of the tiller, since it will have no effect.

hard burst of power with the rudder full over will turn the boat a lot but move her forward very little.

Turning short round

This is far less of a problem with a short keeled boat than it is with a long keel, modern yachts being able to turn so sharply that traditional three-point turns are rarely necessary. If you do have to make one, remember that prop

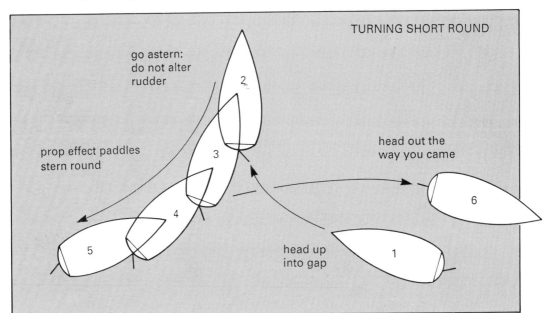

TURNING SHORT ROUND

go astern:
do not alter
rudder

prop effect paddles
stern round

head out the
way you came

head up
into gap

⌂ The right-handed propeller on this boat pulls her stern sharply to port while slowing her down. Then, with the rudder still hard over, a final kick ahead spins her right around and sends her back the way she came.

effect is greater when going astern so make your turn such that you utilise it during the reversing part of the manoeuvre. If the wind or tide can be brought into play then use them, or even a quayside or mooring warp. In strong tides you must be aware of your drift during the time it takes to make a turn. Do not bother

altering the rudder when going astern in a three-point turn, since you do not gather enough way for it to have any effect.

MAINTENANCE

'Out of sight, out of mind' sums up the basic problem with the average yachtsman's attitude to engines. The usual result of this, naturally, is an unreliable engine. This was more understandable in the old days when auxiliary engines were used very little anyway, but

⌂ Just one way of using a mooring warp to manoeuvre in a tight corner.

⌂ You will often be manoeuvring in river currents and strong tidal streams. Use them.

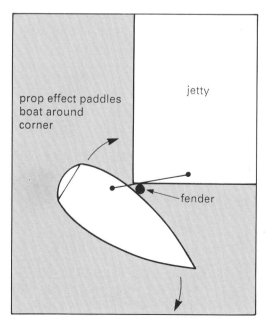

prop effect paddles boat around corner

jetty

fender

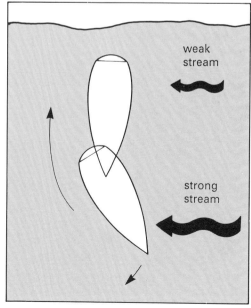

weak stream

strong stream

these days the cruising skipper just cannot afford to be so neglectful – partly because of the horrendous cost of repairs, and partly because harbours and marinas and even rivers are now so crowded that it is often just not safe to enter them without reliable engine power.

Engine maintenance is a relatively simple matter these days, and you should find all the details in your engine manual. Bear in mind the importance of regular checks, not only of oil and water, but also wiring, oil leaks and so on. The vibration of a marine diesel tends to encourage the wiring to disconnect itself, and sea-water is very good at corroding connections. A regular glance over all the wiring and terminals will take only a few moments, but could save a great deal of trouble; the same goes for careful inspection for oil leaks.

One very common problem is the rope around the prop. This is best solved by prevention: whenever the engine is running you must be extra careful to avoid ropes going overboard. Coil and stow any lines that have served their purpose, and make sure your crew understand the importance of hauling mooring warps smartly aboard after casting off.

However many precautions you take, though, you may still run foul of a line from a fishing float or someone else's mooring. By the time you realize there is something wrong the rope will be well and truly jammed.

Stop the engine – assuming it has not stopped already – and make sure it cannot fire up again by removing the plug leads or (on a diesel) decompressing the cylinders. Then try to unwind the rope by hauling on one end while turning the propshaft 'backwards' by hand. This may work with a hemp rope, but artificial fibres tend to wrap around the shaft and melt into a solid mass which no amount of pulling and turning will shift.

The only solution is to cut it off, using a hacksaw or a serrated blade; a smooth blade is no use, however sharp. Try lashing the blade to a pole such as the boathook, and manipulating it from the dinghy. If this fails you may have to go into the water, but this could be dangerous if there is any kind of a sea running. Tie yourself on – and be careful.

◊ *The Williamson Turn is a virtually foolproof way of returning to a casualty under power.*

MAN OVERBOARD

Man overboard techniques when under power are rather less contentious than those under sail. A modern short-keeled yacht turns so readily under power that a technique is hardly required at all, so long as the initial actions as described on page 21 are performed correctly. As soon as the prop is well clear of the casualty you can simply turn round and go back to pick him up. Precisely how you do this will depend on the sea conditions and the type of boat, but in principle you should think of picking him up amidships, where the deck is lowest, the motion least and the prop a reasonable distance away. It is probably best to hold the boat virtually head to wind so that she cannot drift or get thrown onto the casualty by a wave, but at the same time you create a slight lee for him. Shut off the engine completely the moment you get alongside, to prevent his legs being caught in the prop. As with man overboard under sail, you should experiment with different methods for returning to the man overboard, approaching and picking him up. When you have a good, reliable one that suits you, stick to it and practice it.

With a bigger, less manoeuvrable boat you could consider the traditional Williamson Turn, as shown in the diagram. This is similar in principle to the RYA reaching method for sailing boats in that it is simple, reliable, involves no dramatics and is designed to return the boat automatically to the man in the water.

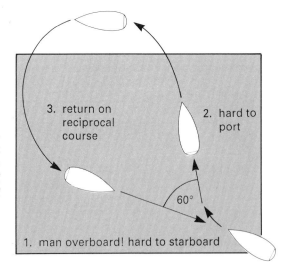

3. return on reciprocal course

2. hard to port

60°

1. man overboard! hard to starboard

8 Berthing alongside

Much of the time the skipper of a cruising yacht carries on his business far from the gimlet eyes of quayside critics. However, unless he contrives to enter all his harbours in the dead of night or the depths of winter he is unlikely to escape their notice when berthing. This is the time when he must handle both boat and crew well if he is to avoid embarrassment.

As ever, the secret of success is organisation of the crew. If you want something doing then you must order a specific person to do that specific job. 'Jane, fender by the chainplate, quick!' is a great deal more efficient than 'Fender over there, someone!'

PREPARING TO BERTH

Before you make the final approach to your berth, think carefully about all the problems that could arise and prepare for them. For example, if you think you may have difficulty getting your stern in, have a forespring standing by led from amidships. You can secure this ashore and go ahead against it with the helm over to swing her in. If you think you might not actually reach the quay, have a heaving line ready so that you can get lines ashore from a

⌂ A quarter rope surged around a cleat will stop you without pulling the stern in.

distance and haul yourself in. Rig your fenders where you think you will need them, but always have at least one mobile fender that can be placed anywhere instantly if needed. If you think you may not be able to stop on arrival – entering a lock with poor astern power and a strong following wind, perhaps – then rig a quarter rope as shown above. Get this secured ashore as soon as possible and it will stop you smoothly if required. Rigged from the quarter like this rather than the stern, it slows you without yanking the stern in.

⌂ With an offshore wind blowing the boat off, a forespring is secured to a cleat aft of the bow.

Motoring ahead against the spring moves the boat steadily sideways and alongside.

During the final approach to a berth keep a good lookout for things that might suddenly and dangerously throw you off track. You may hit a pronounced swirl in the water outside a lockgate that has very recently opened, for example, and some harbours experience a strong surge in certain conditions which can carry you bodily with it as though you are surfing. Either of these could cause you to completely lose control of the boat. Less serious, but still alarming, are sudden violent gusts of wind funnelling through gaps between hills or buildings, equally sudden and violent cross-tides at the ends of quays, or swirls and back-eddies in bays and corners. In some harbours moored dinghies with long doubled mooring warps to shore can be a particular hazard to propellers.

Take your time with this inspection of the approach. If necessary, stand off or heave-to well clear of the berth and make a thorough check through binoculars, watching for these problems as well as the movement of other boats and so on. Do not proceed into the berth until you are certain that all is well, and that you have a clear picture of all the likely difficulties.

⌂ With her bow pointing into the current, the boat is held steady by a headrope and backspring while the other mooring ropes are sorted out.

⌂ Get all the fenders rigged and the warps prepared in good time.

With the crew standing by with the head and stern ropes, approach at roughly 30° to the line of the pontoon.

Don't let your crew jump ashore unless the boat is actually drifting away.

◁ *If you're shorthanded, take both head and stern ropes amidships, stop the boat alongside, step ashore and secure them.*

You must also think carefully about which warps to secure first on arrival at the berth. In a strong tidal stream, for instance, you should secure the headrope and backspring first so that the boat lies reasonably square and steady while you get the others made fast. In a strong offshore wind the headrope is most urgent, but the risk of failing to get the stern in is such that the shore end of the sternrope should be taken right forward, outside all the rigging, so it can be got ashore from the bow. The stern can then be hauled into the berth without panic.

BERTHING UNDER POWER

Many of the cramped and crowded havens we find today actually ban the manoeuvring of large boats under sail, so most of your berthing will be carried out under engine. This should be no problem to the skipper of an efficient, modern yacht, so long as he understands the behaviour of his particular installation. The illustrations on these pages show the basic techniques for berthing under power, both with and without a crew.

Once alongside, the crew can step ashore with the head and stern ropes...

... and take them to suitable cleats on the pontoon. With the boat secure you can switch off the engine...

... and pass the forespring and backspring to the crew to complete the job.

Strong winds and tidal streams make berthing much more difficult, since they carry the boat rapidly off track and into trouble. Despite this they do not really alter the principle of a technique. Take your time studying the conditions around the berth, then keep a very close check on drift by taking transits all round the boat during the approach. If things get out of control do not hesitate to abort and pull out along your escape route.

BERTHING UNDER SAIL

This is usually a good deal more difficult than berthing under power – which is why many port authorities discourage it. The two basic problems that you face are your inability to sail directly into the wind, and your inability to go astern and stop. Having got alongside you then face possible problems with booms and sheets hooking round the quay, the bollards and so on. Berthing alongside under sail needs to be thought out rather more carefully than berthing under power.

Having said all that it is far from impossible, and the diagrams show the basic techniques you can use in a variety of situations. The general principle is to sail close enough and in such a direction that you can hand sails and coast in under momentum; that solves the problems of sheets catching round bollards, and being unable to spill wind at the crucial moment.

Strong winds and tides produce the problems outlined in the previous section, but added to these are the problems of excessive speed and handling sails in a blow. If you are faced with particularly difficult conditions do not be afraid to anchor temporarily on a short scope just off the berth, row your warps ashore and then haul the boat alongside.

MOORING UP

It is useful to consider the purposes of the four basic ropes that hold a boat alongside, for each has a specific function; the boat is not simply tethered to the quay like a horse.

In principle, the headrope holds the bow into the quay, the sternrope holds the stern in, and the springs prevent the boat from moving fore and aft along the quay. To allow for movement caused by the tidal range or wave motion the head and stern ropes need to be led ashore

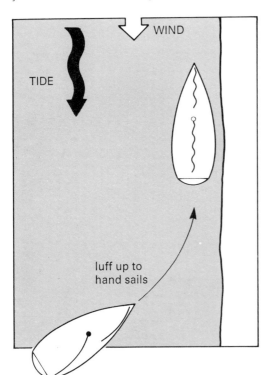

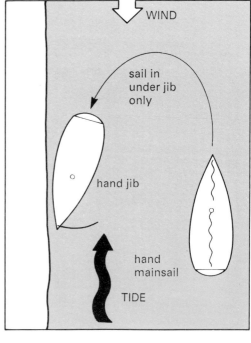

⌂ The yacht properly moored, with headrope, sternrope, forespring and backspring holding her steady and secure.

at about 45 degrees to the quay, and left rather slack. Always rig springs from bow and stern, and lead them as far along the quay as possible. You can then haul them taut to prevent surging, yet still allow for movement in tide and waves.

Springs rigged from amidships are quite useless when berthed in a tideway as they will not hold the boat square in the stream. Without a spring to the stern the boat will fall back onto her headrope in the stream, which will then pull the bow hard into the quay. When the tide runs the other way a forespring from the bow is needed to keep her stern out.

You will need to adjust the warps at times, and this makes it extremely bad practice to use one rope for more than one job (the tail of a headrope as a spring, for example) or one cleat for more than one rope. Every mooring warp should be a separate rope, led to its own cleat. You can then adjust any one of them without interfering with the others (which in rough conditions may not be safe, or even possible).

When rafting alongside another boat, put extra head and stern ropes to the shore so that the warps from the other craft do not have to take the weight of both boats. Run these as far along the quay as you can, so that they also

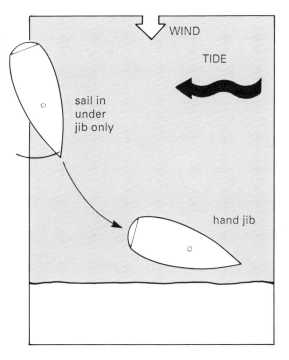

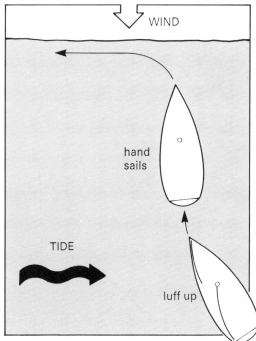

take some of the weight off the other boat's springs. Secure your boat so the mast is clear of the other's or the spreaders might tangle.

The golden rule when mooring up is to ask yourself: 'If I get whisked off by a flying saucer for a month, am I certain the boat will be all right on my return?' If the answer is 'yes', then you can relax in the pub and sleep easily in your bed.

◊ *If you need to anchor stern-to, take care not to foul the tackle of other boats. Motor up, let go the anchor, then motor forward against the anchor to spin her into position for backing in.*

◇ *Stern-to mooring can be tricky. With a right-handed prop you should back in as shown below, taking the headrope aft and securing it to the buoy as you pass it.*

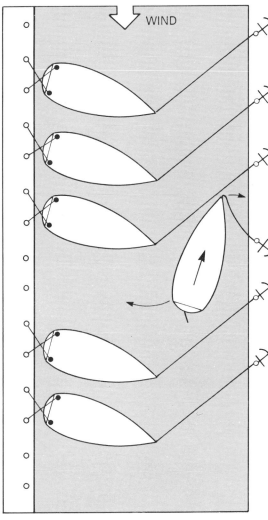

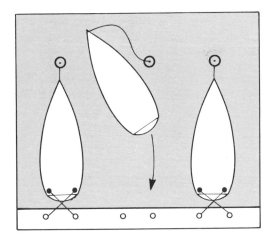

◇ *Springing out of a tight marina berth. Rig the headrope and backspring as slip ropes to each end of the pontoon, and motor slowly aft.*

The crew ease the slip ropes gradually to keep the boat under control. The headrope stops the wind blowing her bow into the neighbouring boat.

CREW SAFETY

If things do not go exactly right when berthing alongside, the warps can often come under tremendous strain. Ropes can part, fittings can break or pull out of the deck, all with extremely unpleasant consequences for anyone standing in the way. A parting wire hawser, for example, can quite literally cut a man in half.

You may not have wire hawsers on your yacht, but the basic dangers remain. Ensure that crew do not stand anywhere that could put them in danger if a warp under strain parts, slips or breaks something. Coils can tighten round a leg and break it or worse; leading blocks can give way allowing a warp to flick sideways and jam a crewman against a wall or a mast. Think of the danger areas and make sure your crew keep clear of them.

↪ *As a mooring rope tightens round his ankle, this crewman could lose his balance, his foot or even his life. Where is his knife?*

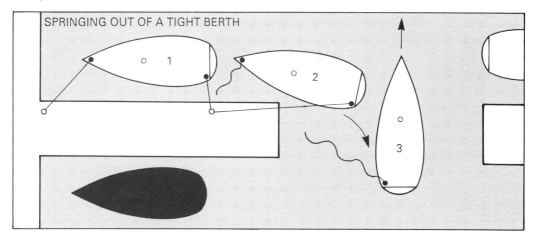

SPRINGING OUT OF A TIGHT BERTH

↪ *As soon as the bow is clear, slip the headrope. Meanwhile secure the backspring aboard the boat to act as a pivot. Keep motoring aft.*

Once it has pulled the stern round far enough, slip the backspring, haul it aboard and engage forward gear. You're away!

9 Anchoring and mooring

There are three distinct aspects of anchoring: choosing an anchorage, selecting a suitable berth in that anchorage, and letting go the anchor in such a way that you ensure you stay there.

CHOOSING AN ANCHORAGE

The two most important requirements are shelter from wind and shelter from waves. Short waves directly generated by the wind will not go round corners, so an anchorage sheltered from the wind will also be protected from these waves. But long swells left over from a previous or distant wind will often bend round into an apparently sheltered anchorage and make it quite untenable.

High ground around an anchorage may seem to provide the best shelter, but 'falling' winds howling down the lee slopes of mountains may combine with the funnelling effect of valleys to create vicious squalls that can drag even the most firmly embedded ground tackle. The best shelter is provided by trees, which filter the wind and prevent squalls and back-eddies.

⇨ Finding an anchor berth among tightly moored boats is not at all easy. Take your time.

Waves probably present the greatest danger to an anchored boat, because as the boat rides up on a wave the cable snubs up taut, loosening the anchor. Waves can even be a problem in rivers when strong wind-against-tide conditions prevail in long open stretches. Try to anchor clear of the tidal stream.

The holding ground is also an important consideration, so you should always check the nature of the bottom on the chart. Rock and weed both make for poor holding, especially with modern anchors. Use a tripping line in rock, and also if you suspect foul ground. Keep well clear of underwater cables, oyster beds and so on; these should all be clearly marked on the chart.

Passing commercial traffic in a river can be a danger to anchored yachts, partly because of wash snubbing the cable and partly because of the risk of collision. Anchor well clear of the main channel and always set a riding light: a single white light showing all around (for a vessel less than 50 metres long). By day you should rig a single anchor ball (if you are using a mooring the pick-up buoy hoisted up the forestay is adequate).

SELECTING A BERTH

Having chosen a safe, comfortable and secure anchorage you must now decide precisely where to anchor. This can be a problem in a crowded anchorage, owing to the difficulty of assessing the swinging room required by all the other boats. With many different types of boat, some anchored on chain and some on rope, and probably all on different scopes of cable, it is very hard to visualise exactly how they will behave. If others are secured to permanent moorings the difficulties are multiplied. There is also the risk of draping your cable across that of a neighbour.

The tightest swinging circle will be that of a moored boat, then a heavy boat anchored on chain. A light boat on rope will sail about all

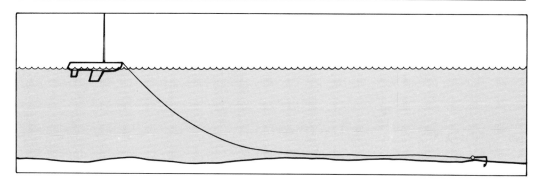

over the anchorage in any wind and should be given a very wide berth. Try to visualise the positions of nearby boats' anchors, and also how you will all swing when the tide turns. Bear in mind that a boat may lie to a bight of cable when she swings away from her anchor, and could actually be sitting over the top of her anchor at some states of the tide. Do not be afraid to make a couple of slow passes through the anchorage while you appraise the situation. It is better to spend a little time doing this than have to weigh anchor and move berth at 0200 in the rain, as the tide turns and puts your bowsprit through another boat's porthole.

When calculating depths in the berth make sure there will be sufficient at Low Water throughout your projected stay. If the tides are making up to Springs, the depth at Low Water may decrease noticeably over a couple of days. Also ensure that there will be sufficient

▱ *As the tide turns you will swing round on the cable, and may end up on top of your anchor.*

▱ *Ideally, your boat should lie to a long scope of cable pulling horizontally on the anchor.*

depth throughout the area of your swinging circle, and leave a good safety margin all round.

ANCHORING THE BOAT

Finally, you must actually let go the anchor and fasten the boat to the seabed as securely as possible, and there is rather more to this than simply slinging the hook over the side. In an ideal world you would lie as in the diagram above, with the full scope of cable pulling horizontally along the sea-bed where it joins the anchor. The length of cable should be at least three or four times the depth with chain, and five or six times the depth with nylon warp; this will maintain the horizontal pull on the anchor and keep it dug in.

You should at least start off like this, even though as the tide turns you will probably at

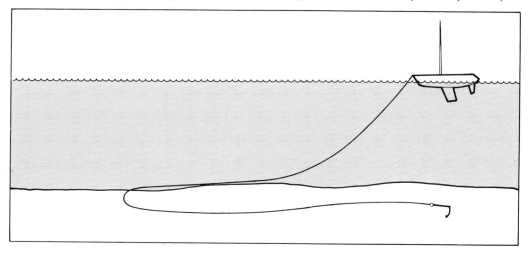

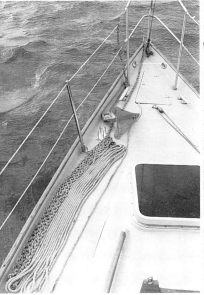

⌂ *Take the cable from the anchor over the rail and back through the bow roller to be flaked on deck.*

This enables the crew to simply pick up the anchor and drop it over the rail when he gets the signal.

Anchor away! As the cable slips out through the bow roller the crew controls it with his foot.

some stage lie to the bight of the chain. The important thing to avoid is piling the chain up in a heap on top of the anchor, as this will both reduce holding power and risk disturbing the set of the anchor as you swing. Whether you let go on the run and sail past the anchor, or stop, let go and drop back, you must control the chain so that it pays out steadily, laying itself along the seabed in a straight line. If you are under power, give a burst with the engine to ensure that the anchor is well dug in.

Unless circumstances prevent it you should try to lay the cable from the anchor towards danger (shallow water, rocks) so that you cannot swing any closer later. Also, try to lie to the stronger strain (ebb tide, wind) when the cable is stretched out. If you swing and a strong tide or wind drags the bight straight the set will be disturbed and it could drag.

Having got safely anchored you must ensure

⌂ *Anchoring under sail: approach on the beat while the tackle is prepared.*

The anchoring will be done head to wind, so get the crew to lower the headsail and lash it to the rail.

With the headsail out of the way, the crew stands by with the anchor.

The cable has been flaked in fathom lengths, so the crew can see how much is going out.

Using his fingers in a prearranged signal to the skipper he indicates the length of cable veered.

Controlling the final run with the bow cleat, he indicates which way the cable is leading.

that you stay there. From the navigational standpoint this means taking anchor bearings so that you have a fix of your anchored position and can tell if you drag. You will, of course, swing round the anchor as the tide and wind change, so your position will be a circle rather than a point; your anchor bearings should consist of three clearing bearings to mark the edges of the swinging circle rather than an actual fix.

From the seamanship standpoint the secret of staying where you are is to keep the cable pulling horizontally on the anchor, so that it does not try to lift it out. If the cable tends to rise off the bottom in strong conditions a useful trick is to slide a weight down it to improve the angle of pull. A dragging anchor in wind is usually indicated by the boat lying beam-on to the wind, since the dragging anchor generally allows the wind to blow the bow off.

The other crew member stands by the main halyard, ready to lower the sail.

Let go the anchor, and immediately lower the main to prevent the boat sailing over the anchor.

Stow the main as the boat slips back in the wind and the cable is veered.

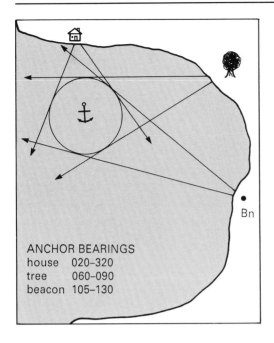

ANCHOR BEARINGS
house   020–320
tree   060–090
beacon 105–130

CLEARING A FOULED ANCHOR

If you hook your anchor around a chain or cable, try to heave it to the surface. Pass a slip rope around the fouled cable and secure it on board; lower the anchor until it is clear, then haul it up to the stemhead. You can then slip the cable.

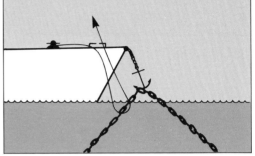

MOORING THE BOAT

The advantages of this rather than anchoring are that you are extremely unlikely to drag, and you do not have all the difficulty of selecting a berth. But do check with the yacht club or harbourmaster that the mooring is free to use, and do haul up the riser and inspect the shackle holding it to the buoy for wear or corrosion; ensure that the riser is big enough for your boat. Secure the boat to the ring of the buoy with chain or a shackle or a tight couple of round turns of rope so as to prevent chafe; never moor with a slip-rope as the boat's movement

⟲ With wind against tide, lower the main to approach under headsail only.

One crew indicates the direction of the mooring buoy while the others stow the mainsail on the boom.

Let the jib flap to slow the boat as the buoy comes within range.

⌂ Ideally, one crew lies holding a pick-up rope while the other indicates where the buoy is.

With the mooring buoy almost under the bow, the crewman lying on deck gets ready to check the state of the riser and the shackle beneath the buoy.

All being well he rigs the pick-up rope and prepares to moor up to the eye of the buoy with chain.

will chafe it and could cut through it overnight. Use a slip-rope to get a line onto the buoy, then leave it on loosely as a back-up to the main line – and also in readiness for slipping when you leave.

Mooring between piles is necessary in many harbours and this has to be done with some care in strong tides or winds, or you risk losing control of one end of the boat.

If you are properly equipped you can lay your own mooring with two anchors. When space is limited this has the considerable benefit of reducing your swinging circle to roughly that of the boats on moorings. It also

With the boat more or less stopped the crew can grab the pick-up buoy.

In a strong tide, sheet the jib in to hold the boat on station while the mooring chain is hauled aboard.

With all secure the jib can be lowered and stowed while the boat drops back.

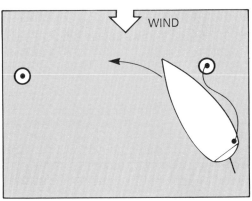

⌂ *Mooring between piles in a cross-wind: Bring the stern line forward and secure it to the first pile before motoring across to the other one.*

avoids the problem of dragging the bight round and upsetting a single anchor, which is most useful if you have to leave the boat for a period.

The principle of laying a mooring is quite simple: let go one anchor, then either proceed beyond it or drop back from it until you have laid twice the calculated required scope. Then let go the second anchor, and shorten the first cable as you let out the second until they are equal. Seize the two cables together with a tight racking seizing outside the bow and lower the join well below your keel.

The anchors should be laid up and down the stream, the heavier one holding you against the greater strain (usually the ebb tide, or wind).

⌂ *A good solid mooring: two hefty nylon pendants with spliced-in hard eyes are shackled to the ring of the buoy, which is hauled up tight against the bow fender to reduce chafe. The shackles are moused with wire and the anchor chain is left clear for instant use, just in case.*

⋄ *How to lay your own mooring.*

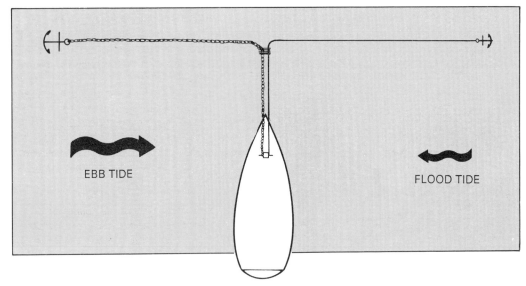

10 A day sail

It's time to go sailing. Let us imagine we keep our boat – a 28-foot bermudan sloop – in a marina on the south side of a sheltered tidal estuary. It is Tuesday afternoon and we have decided, my wife and I, to take our two children out sailing on Saturday, weather permitting. How do we go about this apparently simple project?

DECIDING WHETHER TO SAIL

Even for just a day sail you should note the developing pattern of the weather for some days beforehand, if only so you can abandon the trip in good time for everyone to plan something else if the weather looks to be turning foul.

Much of the time this decision – to sail or not to sail – is relatively easy where a day sail is concerned, but sooner or later you will be faced with that horrid 'south-west 5 to 6, rain at times, visibility moderate or poor' that puts you in a quandary. You can be sure that some of the crew will rejoice at the prospect of a hard thrash to windward, while others will groan inwardly but refuse to admit that they would rather spend the afternoon watching the tennis on TV. You may fancy watching the tennis yourself, particularly if you have had a tiring week, but you should try very hard to shelve your personal feelings and consider the overall benefit to your crew of sailing or not, especially if young children are involved who are not in a position to withhold their labour when you unwisely decide to sail on a bad forecast.

To sail or not is probably the most difficult decision facing a new skipper and it is a wise one who errs on the side of caution until he has found his feet. Remember the saying: 'Any fool can go to sea, but it takes a seaman to stay in harbour'. The inference should be obvious.

PREPARING FOR A SAIL

It is tempting to be a little slapdash when preparing for an apparently simple day sail, but it is a temptation that must be strenuously resisted. Even a short trip down the river and back can last an awfully long time if you do your tidal sums wrong and end up having to beat against the tide for a few miles in a lumpy estuary chop just as night is falling and the temperature starts to plummet. Errors like these can easily ruin the day for everyone, and if the crew get cold, tired and fed-up they are very likely to make mistakes when handling sails, berthing and so on.

◊ *Before deciding to set sail, use your eyes. A small yacht coming in with double-reefed main and well-rolled genoa is a sure sign that it's windy out there...*

⌂ *If your planning is good the crew will stay cheerful, come what may.*

To prevent this you need a passage plan – for a day sail is just a short passage, after all. You need to consider where you are going, your route, alternatives in case the weather changes, tides and a host of other factors – all covered in some detail in the next section. You must also ensure that the crew are equipped with food and hot drinks, towels, changes of clothes, wind-proof jackets, foul-weather gear, sun-tan lotion and so on, and that the boat is properly equipped and prepared for sea.

SAILING OUT

Having briefed the crew on what to bring, prepared the boat and checked the weather forecasts, you decide on Friday evening that all is well for the morrow. Unless there really is no point in leaving too early because of a foul tide, you should get everyone up and aboard as early as you can so as to make the most of the day. Early morning in the summer is a glorious time of day and there are few who will not ultimately thank you for dragging them out of their beds to experience it – but make sure you are there to greet them with a cheerful, smiling face and a whistling kettle as the sun creeps over the horizon.

Having studied the weather and related it to what was forecast you should have planned where to go for the day, and can now discuss it with your bleary-eyed crew over coffee. Always aim in principle to come home with the tide under you, so that whatever may happen to the wind or your engine, the boat will make her way homewards anyway at going-home time. A long, late and slow flog back to your berth over a strengthening spring ebb is no way to round off a long and enjoyable, but probably tiring day. If you make a habit of it you will very quickly find crews in short supply!

Within the limitations imposed by ensuring a good trip home at the end of the day you should endeavour to cram as much into the day as you can. This does not necessarily mean furious physical activity. Your friends may be quite happy just sailing along or lying about sunbathing, but youngsters especially need to be kept occupied with a variety of events. Tack, gybe, change sails, anchor for lunch, send them away in the dinghy to explore the nearby beach, and if all else fails get them to do some simple maintenance around the boat.

SAILING HOME

If you have travelled a long way then start home in good time; you can always slow down or make a detour as you get closer and are able to calculate more accurately and reliably your ETA at the berth. Start clearing up, cleaning down, stowing and packing before your arrival, especially if you are running late. Make a list of victuals required for the next trip and check the fuel and water. If you are under sail, run the engine for a while to charge the batteries right up. In other words, aim to arrive at the berth with the boat all ready to go sailing again. You can then all step straight ashore and go home; you, the skipper, armed with a complete list of requirements for the next trip.

This may sound somewhat super-organised for what is supposed to be a casual day out sailing. However, bearing in mind that the crew are likely to be cold and tired by their return, you can boost morale considerably by being ready to zip straight off home after berthing. All too many skippers mess about for another hour while the crew stand around making mental notes never to sail on that boat again. Enthusiasm wears thin at the end of a good day, when the fun is deemed to be over. Do not spoil things for your crew by dragging your heels.

PART THREE

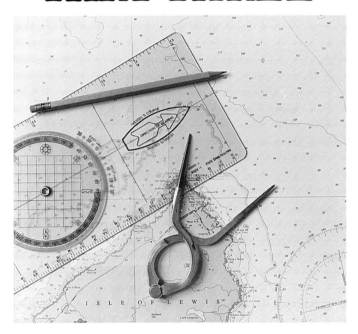

MAKING A
PASSAGE

Sailing a yacht for the day requires many qualities of you as a skipper, but cruising proper – making passages offshore or along the coast – is the real meat and drink of a cruising skipper's business. It is only when making a passage that you truly 'walk alone', with no nearby home to run to when things get sticky, no comforting, familiar landmarks to encourage and reassure you, and few nearby vessels to assist you.

On a passage of any length you must also get some sleep, which means you need to trust your crew implicitly. You must be able to close your eyes knowing that the crew in charge can be relied on to keep the yacht safe in your absence. Your crew must respect you sufficiently to obey your every command even when you are not there to see it carried out. Failure to take proper charge of a vessel on a day sail may do little more than make the crew complain about you on their return home. Failure to do so on a passage could mean that they – and you – do not return home at all.

This section of the book deals with the aspects of skippering that make the difference between a successful passage and one that is merely survived, or perhaps not even that.

11 Planning the passage

You can often start the overall planning of a summer cruise as far back as the previous winter. This type of long-term planning clearly cannot be detailed, but it does help you decide on the general area you wish to sail in and alerts you to the difficulties you may encounter en route.

You should undertake the more detailed planning of a specific passage perhaps a day or two before sailing, having studied the weather pattern over a period and decided to positively undertake the trip, barring last-minute snags. There are various aspects to this business of planning, the first being a careful analysis of the passage's component parts.

ANALYSING THE PASSAGE

Most offshore and coastal passages can be considered as three separate stages:

1 Getting clear of the departure harbour, and into a position from which you can set a course to the destination.
2 Sailing to a convenient point outside the approaches to the destination.
3 Approaching and entering the destination harbour.

The first and the third involve pilotage, while the middle bit is navigation; there is an important difference, and the planning of a passage is much simplified by separating it into these three sections.

Make a start on planning the passage by reading carefully the relevant pilot books, not only for detailed information on the harbours concerned, but also for tidal and other information relevant to the actual passage. Having absorbed this you can then study the charts, paying particular attention to any dangers marked or noted along the track. The clearer your mental picture of the passage at this stage, the easier you will find the actual navigation and pilotage when you might be cold, tired and seasick.

You should also prepare rough plans, and make sure you have charts and pilot books for alternative harbours if the weather prevents you making the chosen one. Even if your chosen harbour is accessible in all conditions you must consider the possibility of having to abandon it for other reasons such as lack of time, crew seasickness or weariness, or strong headwinds.

Study and record the weather forecasts for some days beforehand, so you get a clear picture of the way the weather is developing. If time is limited, you can then look ahead to the likely weather prevailing when you want to return, and choose a harbour that will give you a good passage home. This is usually more important than a good passage out – not only because you may have a job to return to, but also because your crew's enthusiasm for hard sailing may have waned by the end of the cruise.

⇨ If you plan your passage well in advance you will have less to do when you get to sea.

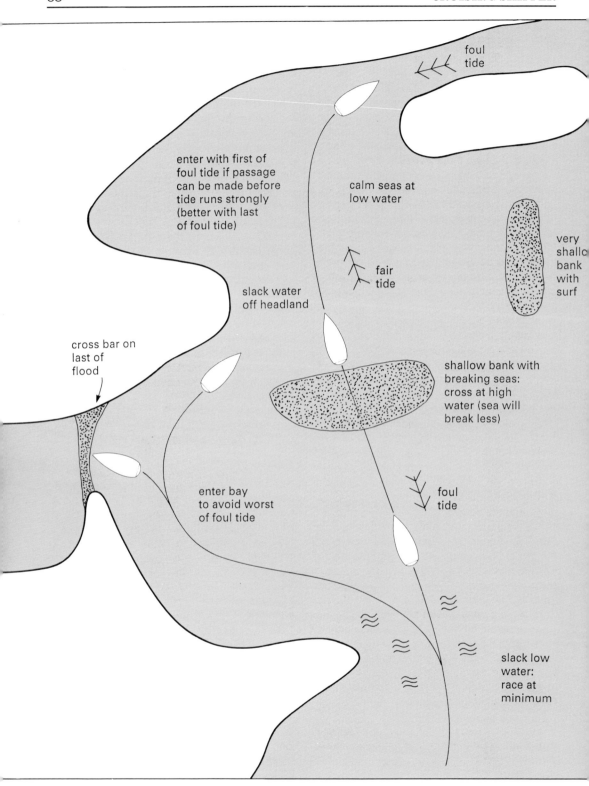

foul
tide

enter with first of
foul tide if passage
can be made before
tide runs strongly
(better with last
of foul tide)

calm seas at
low water

very
shallo
bank
with
surf

fair
tide

slack water
off headland

cross bar on
last of
flood

shallow bank with
breaking seas:
cross at high
water (sea will
break less)

enter bay
to avoid worst
of foul tide

foul
tide

slack low
water:
race at
minimum

With a general plan worked out you can now turn to the detailed planning of your outward passage. The two most important factors involved in this are leaving at the right time and going in the right direction; to both of which there is a good deal more than meets the eye. Let us consider the question of timing first.

TIMING THE PASSAGE

Inevitably there will be certain places in a passage which are best negotiated at certain times, and perhaps some that *must* be negotiated at certain times. You can rarely plan a passage to accommodate them all, so you will have to compromise. The first thing to do is to list all the parts of the passage which will be affected by timing, then sort them into priorities. The likely factors are:

• Any limiting tidal height needed for leaving, due to a drying berth, marina sill, river bar etc.

• Any limiting times for leaving due to difficult or dangerous tidal streams, breaking seas on a bar, lack of shore lights, the need to see drying banks for navigation, and so on.

• The need to pass through races, overfalls or narrow channels, or around headlands at a particular state of the tide.

• The need to carry a fair tide along a coast, or lee-bow a tide across a channel, during certain stages of the passage.

• The desirability of crossing busy shipping lanes in daylight.

• The preference for making an initial landfall at night, when coastal lights are visible for easy fixing.

• The need or desire to approach and enter harbour in daylight.

• Tidal height or stream limitations on approaching and entering the destination harbour, as in the first three points above.

• Whether a few hours delay will allow the current weather pattern to change to a more favourable one; the passage of a cold front, for example, changing murky south-westerly conditions into clear north-westerly ones.

◊ *Analyze your proposed passage for stages that will be affected by timing, then list these in order of priority. Be ready to change your plans, and leave a margin for error.*

There are a great many factors here, and it is important to deal with them methodically if you are to make any sense of them all. Consider the relative importance of each, and the knock-on effects of alternative timings (such as leaving a drying berth on the flood or the next ebb) right through the passage.

If, for example, you are limited to leaving a marina up to half tide but have no element of danger (such as a breaking bar) to contend with, you may find that staying in your cosy bunk for an extra three or four hours until the ebb may enable you to catch a fair tide round a troublesome headland, or lee-bow a channel tide before tacking towards a windshift (see next section). On a simpler level, there is little point in flogging away to arrive off a small unlit port at midnight, then having to heave-to until dawn, if you can stay in the pub for the evening and go off at first light on a 24-hour passage. But you must always bear in mind the uncertainty of accurately timing any passage under sail. Give yourself a margin of error; you do not want to arrive at a lock gate half an hour after it shuts, with a rising onshore gale and night falling.

SETTING THE COURSE

With a fair wind to your destination, forecast to remain so for the duration of the passage, all you need do is calculate the course to steer, point the boat in that direction, set the sails and put the kettle on. If the wind begins fair, but is forecast to shift ahead, it might benefit you to set course towards one side of your destination so that you avoid having to beat when the wind shifts. This will require some thought, since it will not always be worthwhile. You will need to weigh up the extra time sailed against the time that might be saved by maintaining a free wind when it shifts. A few sums, some careful weather forecasting, and some geometry will be needed here.

If the wind is inconsiderate enough to be on the nose at the start of the passage, and forecast to remain there, you have three basic ways of dealing with it. The first is to make just two long tacks; the second is to make a number of short tacks; and the third is to go somewhere else – you are, after all, cruising for pleasure!

The first approach minimises the effort and delay caused by frequent tacking, as well as simplifying navigation, but you do risk overstanding your destination when tacking in from a long leg. If the wind shifts you risk being caught dead downwind, just as you are about to stand in on the final leg, or massively overstanding your destination if it frees you. If all goes well, however, it is quicker than short tacking.

The short tacking option removes the risk of overstanding and of being caught downwind in a shift, but does involve more navigation and a greater accumulation of navigational inaccuracies, as well as being slower in theory. On the face of it the choice would seem to be a gamble

▽ Short-tacking close to your destination.

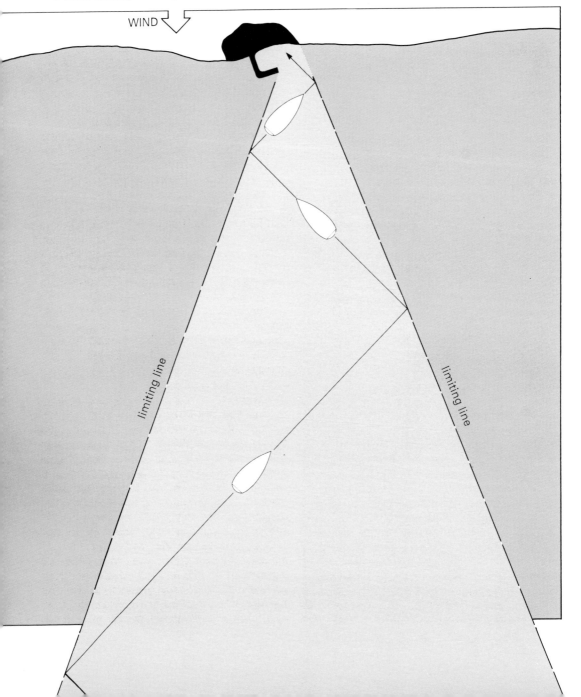

WIND

limiting line

limiting line

on the risky efficiency of two long tacks or the slow and fiddly safety of a number of short tacks. The decision as to which approach to adopt is, however, frequently dictated by factors other than personal preference. Let us look at them.

You can greatly reduce the risk of overstanding the destination with two long tacks by

▷ *Taking advantage of a windshift.*

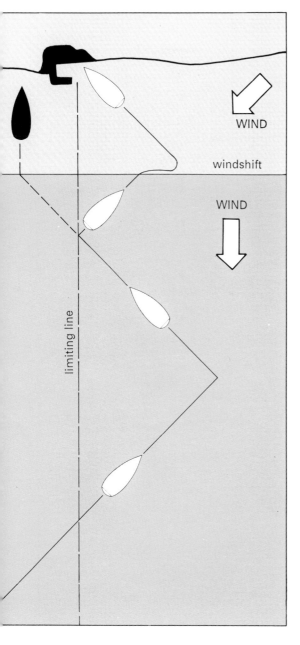

WIND

windshift

WIND

limiting line

putting in the second tack early, producing in effect a passage of three tacks. With a steady wind that is forecast to maintain its direction, this is probably the best course, combining the advantages of both long and short tacking. It is particularly suitable for a small or weak crew, a boat that is slow in stays, or very strong winds in which tacking would be especially wearisome and time-consuming. If the wind is erratic, creating a danger of being caught downwind at the end of a tack, then you can gradually increase the number of tacks from this ideal until they produce a passage that is close enough to the track to ease your mind. If you gradually reduce the lengths of the tacks as you approach your destination this will reduce the risk of being caught downwind of your goal by a windshift, and also of overstanding.

If the wind is forecast to shift to a particular direction during the passage, start with a single long tack towards the direction of the expected shift. When the shift comes, the boat will be strongly headed and you can tack immediately to take full advantage of the weather gauge that has now been gained. You will need to judge the time of the expected shift carefully, because you could seriously overstand your goal if it comes late. If you plot a limiting line back from the destination which represents the course you can sail close-hauled in the new wind, it will indicate how far you can safely sail away at any stage of the passage without the risk of overstanding when the wind shifts. If you then make your tacks between this line and the new wind direction, you can be sure of a free wind when it comes.

If you experience reasonably strong tidal streams from abeam or thereabouts during the passage, then by and large you should time your tacks so that the tide is always setting up from leeward, underneath the lee bow. This is known as lee-bowing the tide, and it has two benefits: it keeps the boat close to the direct track (in case of windshifts) and it enables you to point higher and sail faster owing to the increase in apparent wind caused by the tide pushing you towards the wind. But this should not normally take priority over sailing towards a windshift for a free wind usually produces greater benefits than that gained by lee-bowing the tide. If the windshift is expected late, however, you can profitably set up your initial tacks to take full advantage of lee-bowing effects before finally standing off towards the shift.

You can make huge savings in time and effort by planning and executing a passage according to these principles. The key to the whole thing, as ever, is the weather; not one of these tactics is worth twopence unless your weather fore-casting is accurate, and I cannot stress too much the value of recording and studying a sequence of forecasts some days before setting off. It is the only way to get a real feel for the way the weather pattern is developing.

▷ *Tacking during a cross-channel passage to keep the tide on the lee bow.*

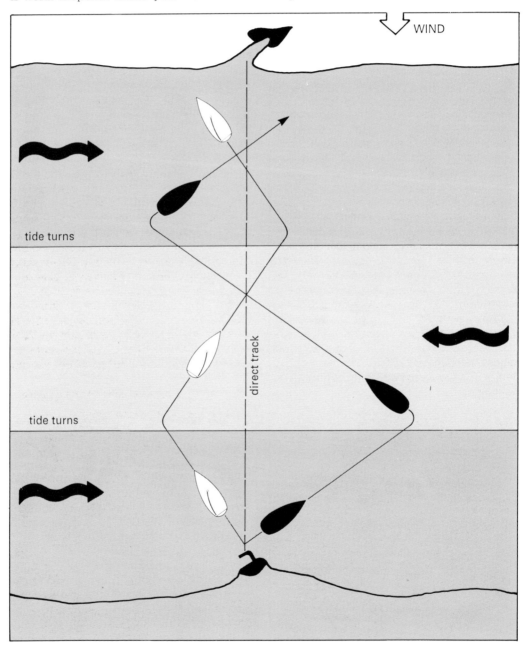

12 Navigation on passage

The realities of navigating a cruising yacht on passage are usually a long way from the theories of the classroom. The sheer practical difficulties of navigating in bad weather, consumed with exhaustion and seasickness, cannot be exaggerated. Unfortunately, neither can the importance of it, and we must face the fact that the more difficult the conditions for navigation, the more important its accuracy becomes.

Accuracy in this context, however, is not the same thing as accuracy in a classroom. Theoretical textbook accuracy is not only quite impossible at sea in a small boat, but can in fact be positively dangerous. It may be perfectly feasible to plot a course to steer of 332½ degrees, but it will be quite impossible to steer it. If the navigator writes down 332½ often enough there is a serious risk of him believing that his boat is actually sailing in that direction, and she won't be. No small boat can be steered to a greater accuracy than the nearest five degrees, and all courses should be rounded off accordingly. Not only will this enable the helmsman to hold the compass lubber line against a big clear black triangle on the compass card, but it will also instill in everyone's minds that 'rounded off to the nearest five degrees' is the sort of accuracy applicable to navigation.

A most important aid to accuracy is the minimising of unnecessary errors such as incorrect calculations, illegible figures and lost bits of paper. A tidy chart table, a navigator's notebook for jottings, and a tidy mind are simple ways of eliminating potential problems. The only object that should lie on the chart table is the chart; everything else should have its own special stowage place, and be kept there.

THE DR PLOT

The dead reckoning plot is the traditional method of small boat navigation and it should still be used today, even if you carry all the electronics known to man. Its merits are simplicity and reliability, yet in the hands of an experienced navigator it can be remarkably accurate. The secrets of running an accurate DR are simplicity and observation. Note the points made above about accuracy, and watch what is happening. Watch how far from the course ordered the helmsman actually steers; watch the wake and the angle of heel carefully before assessing leeway; consider very carefully any inconsistencies that might be showing

⟳ *Keep it tidy, and you'll make fewer mistakes.*

TIME BST	COURSE ORDERED (°C)	LOG READING	ESTIMATED COURSE STEERED	DIST RUN	LEEWAY	WIND	SEA	WEATHER	Vis	Bar	POSITION	SOURCE OF FIX	NEXT WP	REMARKS	REFUEL	ENG HOURS
0001																
0100																
0200																
0300																
0400																
0500																
0600																
0700	⌕	–	–	–	–	NWS	Calm	⁰/₈	G	15	Denhaven Hr	Vis	–	0740 Start engine		
0800	Var	–	Var	–	–						entrance	vis	1	0750 Slip under power. Co & Sp to clear Hr – WP1 Dep fix		
0900	250	2.7	250	2.7	3°		slight			15½	Griddle Pier	vis	4	0805 WP1. a/c 240. Set full main + gen. Sp 3kts Set log ⌕. Stop engine. 0830 Bench. Bn red 1". L1.2. 0855 Griddle pier ← ½' L25. a/c 250		
1000		6.5		3.8		NW4	mod				54°11.'2N:01°13.4E	RN		0915 wind inc. Red. gen. 09.25 TS now fair		
1100		10.9		4.3	4°						54°10.'1N:01°10.5 E					
1200	185	15.8	190	4.7	nil					16	54°06.'2N:01°09.4E		29	1115 WP4. a/c 185. L120. unfurl Gen		
1300		20.6		4.7							54°01.'1N:01°08.7E			1230 Fix NN		
1400		25.6		4.9				⁵/₈ H			53°55.'0N:01°07.3E					
1500		29.7	185	4.1	5°	WS				17	53°52.'2N:01°05.'2E			1430 wind b. WS. Red. gen. 2 rolls Mn		
1600	160	347	165	4.8	nil						53°50.'1N:01°07.'2E		41	1520 WP29. a/c 160 L 31.8. 1530 Hard Lt v. ↤1'		
1700		40.9	163	6.5		M/R					53°47.'2N:01°09.3E					
1800		47.1	160	6.3		W4		⁵/₈ H			53°44.'5N:01°11.2E			1805 50m contour		
1900		54.0		7.1							53°40.'9N:01°13.'3E			1930 Entered shipping lanes		
2000		60.5	165	6.9		WS					53°38.'2N:01°14.9E					

☞ *Keep the log up to date as a check on your DR.*

up in the log. Keep regular records of all these observations in the logbook for reference, together with details of frequent fixes which you can use to maintain a continuous check on the accuracy of the DR.

One very important benefit of working with a DR plot rather than an electronic navigator is the way a single course can be plotted and sailed over a long period while you are subject to a variety of tidal streams. The classic situation is when crossing a wide channel on, say, a 24-hour passage, when opposing tidal streams are likely to very nearly cancel out. The DR navigator can estimate his passage time, sum

☞ *Use your fixes to check your EPs, and vice versa, and investigate any discrepancies.*

up the total tidal influence during that time and plot a single course allowing for it (assuming he can safely drift back and forth clear of danger). The consequences of any change or slight miscalculation can be allowed for during the final approach. This is a very much more efficient and less time-consuming method of making a passage than constantly having to adjust the course for an electronic navigator's cross-track error.

ELECTRONIC NAVIGATION

In my view a competent skipper should proceed on passage as though everything electronic on board is on the point of collapse. He must say to himself as the fog descends halfway across the shipping lanes 'What do I do if

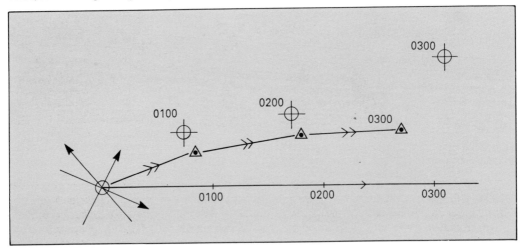

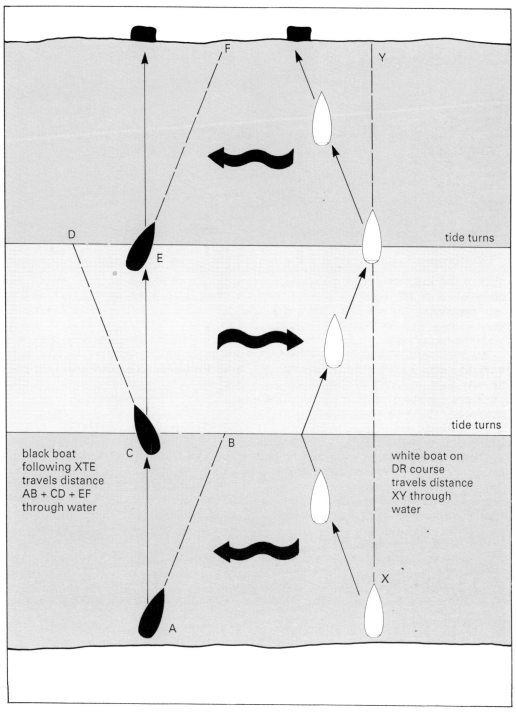

black boat
following XTE
travels distance
AB + CD + EF
through water

white boat on
DR course
travels distance
XY through
water

tide turns

tide turns

⌂ On the face of it, navigating by cross-track error on a cross-channel passage makes for a more direct route (left). But if there are tidal streams running you will be fighting the tide to stay on track. It is much more efficient to drift sideways with the tide while sailing forward across the water (right); if you get your DR plot right you will arrive quicker, with less fuss.

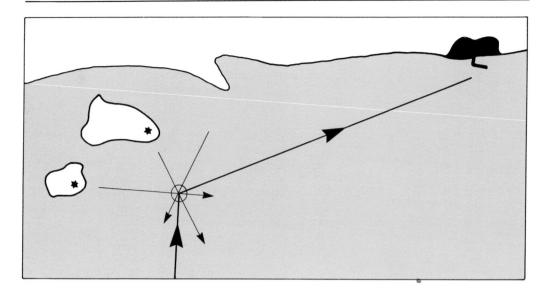

the radar and the GPS set cease working right now?' If he does not have a satisfactory answer to this question then he could easily find himself in serious trouble.

I am not advocating the abolition of electronic navigation aids, merely the application of common sense and good seamanship to their use. In the same way that the airline pilot has contingency plans for electronic failure, so must you. He, of course, has the inestimable advantage of knowing that as he sits wondering what to do next his aeroplane is likely to be plummetting earthwards; this tends to concentrate the mind. You should imagine yourself being converged upon by three or four 30-knot supertankers; which, in certain stretches of water, may well be the case.

By all means bask in the luxury of being able to press a button and know where you are, but don't give up the day-job; keep your DR plot running with all the accuracy you can muster. Use the electronic fixes to check it, and use it to check them.

MAKING A LANDFALL

The difficulty of identifying an unfamiliar coast is such that you should always consider planning to make landfall at a place that is easy to identify accurately, even if it is not precisely where you are bound. Having obtained a good, accurate landfall fix here, you can then pro-

⌂ Arrange to make your landfall at an easily-identified point, uptide of your goal.

ceed along the coast towards your destination confident that you know where you are. This is infinitely preferable to closing an unknown coast with only a vague idea of your position, especially in poor visibility or onshore gales.

A similar concept can be employed even when there are no clearly identifiable features anywhere on the coast. You should calculate your likely navigational errors, then set course to make landfall so far to one side of your destination that, even if all the errors set you the same way, you can still be certain which side of your destination you are (but be sure you make allowance for any inshore dangers along the coast).

Wherever you decide to approach the land the accurate identification of lights and features is essential, and not always as simple as you might think. Although light characteristics, for example, are carefully arranged so that adjacent lights are easily distinguishable, in a rough sea a light will be obscured at times making it difficult to count accurately. The waves may even cause it to show a quite different characteristic, possibly the same as another half a mile away. This may sound highly unlikely but I have experienced it. Accurate timing with a stopwatch is worthwhile as it will show up the slight discrepancies likely to occur in such a situation.

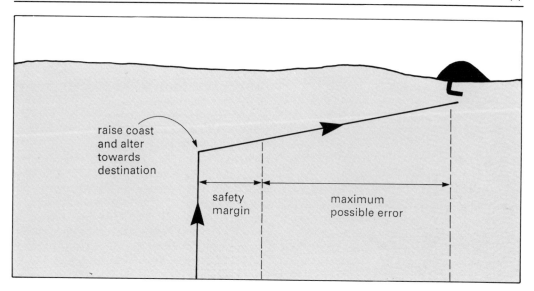

raise coast
and alter
towards
destination

safety
margin

maximum
possible error

If you cannot identify your landfall, make sure you know which side of your goal you are.

Land masses, headlands and hills can often be difficult to identify from certain angles. Headlands, for example, tend to blend into one another when viewed along a coast. Trees (conspic) may have been chopped or blown down, caravan parks may have been moved, while breakwaters that look conspicuous when viewed vertically on a chart may be only 18 inches high, and thus quite invisible from the water. Study the chart and read the pilot book very carefully, and take your time with identifications. Use the compass to 'shoot up' uncertain objects.

Take the trouble to work out a good line of approach, with all the important pilotage features clearly visible.

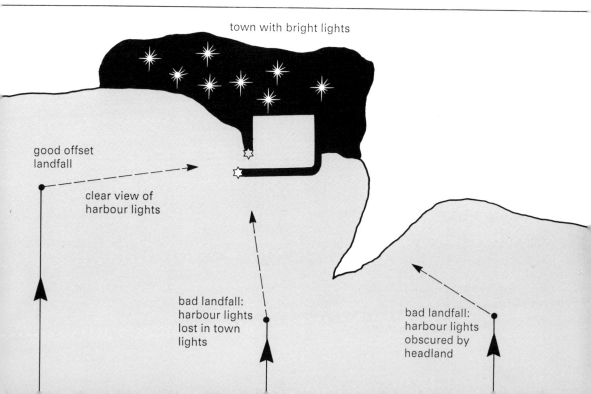

town with bright lights

good offset
landfall

clear view of
harbour lights

bad landfall:
harbour lights
lost in town
lights

bad landfall:
harbour lights
obscured by
headland

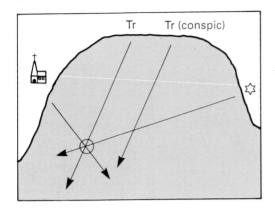

Tr   Tr (conspic)

⌂ *Use your hand-bearing compass to cross-check ambiguous navigation marks.*

There is a tendency to relax on sighting land after a passage, but you should resist this strenuously. This is the difficult bit approaching; far more boats are lost on the land than ever are lost on the sea.

PILOTAGE – BLIND AND VISUAL

The passage from landfall to harbour involves pilotage, a rather specialised type of navigation for restricted waters. The important thing to understand about pilotage is that it tends to tell you where you are not, rather than where you are. In other words, pilotage techniques such as transits, clearing bearings and depth contours all indicate simply that you are clear of a particular charted danger. This, of course, is what concerns you in these waters; you can generally see where you *are* just by looking.

Blind pilotage is the same thing in fog, and it is most important that you have a basic strategy worked out for handling this. Standing around nervously in the cockpit, hoping that some useful landmark will loom out of the murk, is not a strategy. Generally this is one time when it is best for the navigator to stay at the chart table, plotting and planning and sending instructions to the helmsman. The crew on deck need to be carefully briefed as to what to look out for, and how to look out for it.

The comments made earlier about not relying totally on electronic navigators applies especially to blind pilotage. It is essential that you run a plot that is both foolproof and failsafe; if the electronics fail you must be able to switch instantly to using log, lead, lookout and magnetic compass, without loss of concentration or the rhythm of your navigational thoughts.

⌕ *Entering port is not always simple, so plan it.*

ENTERING HARBOUR

Things can happen very quickly when entering the restricted and often confusing confines of a strange harbour. The experienced skipper will have his boat, his crew and himself prepared for coping instantly with any little drama that might crop up.

If you are making for a commercial harbour you need to be able to recognise any lights, shapes and sound signals that you may encounter, and anticipate the tracks likely to be followed by shipping that is under way or clearly about to get under way. The more you can recognise and understand the events that are taking place around you, the more safely and confidently you can make your way through the harbour. The same applies to the other shipping, so ensure that your movements and intentions are at all times quite clear to them. Keep out of the main channels and if necessary use flag signals or VHF to the ships or harbour control.

Entering tricky harbours in difficult conditions can often be simplified by selecting a suitable time. Winding unmarked channels flanked by drying banks are usually best negotiated when there is sufficient water in the channel for you to float safely but insufficient to cover the banks: you can then see the channel clearly. Long narrow harbours subject to powerful tidal streams are best entered around High Water, when streams are slack, water is deep, and the shallows covered sufficiently to effectively widen the entrance. Think about the conditions before blindly charging into a harbour; heaving-to outside for lunch could change a nightmare entry into something your children could handle.

Having got safely inside the harbour you can select your berth using the information in the pilot book, and your own judgement. You can use the VHF radio to organise a marina or harbour berth before your arrival, which simplifies matters greatly. It is then just a matter of securing the boat to it: a problem we have already covered. Report your arrival to the Harbourmaster and check that your berth is suitable for the expected duration of your stay. If you have been abroad there will be customs formalities to deal with, after which you can go ashore for a well-earned rest.

CHECKLIST: ENTERING HARBOUR

● **Clear away anchor and cable ready for use.** This simple precaution could get you out of serious trouble if you lose control of the boat. It also allows you to turn a large boat quickly if you find yourself powering down-tide into a blind alley.

● **Start the engine** and let it run at a fast tickover to warm through. As well as being instantly available, it will also charge the batteries to provide maximum voltage for navigation lights etc, and you will not have to run the engine in the berth.

● **Prepare warps and fenders** so there will be no delay if you have to go alongside somewhere unexpectedly. Keep a short warp available for use as a temporary breastrope for a brief stop.

● **Call the harbourmaster on VHF** to announce your impending arrival and ETA, and to check whether there are any shipping movements that may concern you. If you have no berth organised, ask him for one. Then *keep a listening watch on the port working frequency* to monitor shipping movements and so on.

● **Prepare your pilotage notes well in advance** so that you know exactly what to expect when you enter harbour. Take particular note of any *local entry signals, sound signals, recommended yacht channels* and so on.

13 Watchkeeping routines

As skipper, you should never keep a regular watch unless the boat is sailing very short-handed. This is not a perk, it is simply to ensure that you are always available, refreshed and rested, to attend to any matter that the watchkeepers cannot handle. You will not be able to do this if you spend large parts of the day and night trying to keep awake at the tiller. Do not feel morally obliged to 'stand your trick'. Your most important responsibility to your crew is to be always fully alert in case of emergency.

That said, if you are a family skipper with young children and an inexperienced spouse you will have to be rather more flexible than this if you are to get the necessary rest. Careful study of the navigation and weather situations should enable you to stand watch yourself at difficult times and delegate the watchkeeping when conditions are relatively easy. If a child shares your watch you may well, with suitable precautions and careful briefing, be able to close your eyes now and then in the cockpit. If you need more sleep you should consider heaving-to so that a reliable youngster, securely harnessed to the boat, can keep a lookout for an hour or two in safe open water. Careful preparations like these should enable you to stock up on sleep when circumstances permit, leaving you fresh and rested for when they do not. It is difficult to exaggerate the importance of this.

SELECTING WATCHKEEPERS

The most essential quality in a watchkeeper is reliability. His role is not to run the ship in your absence but simply to keep her safe; he can call you if anything untoward occurs. If you give your instructions carefully a watchkeeper does not need to be very experienced as long as he is sensible and reliable, and can be trusted utterly to call you when he is unsure of anything. You may be up and down the companionway like a yo-yo every time a seagull drifts past in the dark, but your ship will be kept safe.

Briefing

As a watchkeeper's level of experience rises, so can his responsibilities. The young, inexperienced crewman can be told to call the skipper if he sees or hears anything at all, on or off the boat, while the average watchkeeper who has some experience can be given a list of instructions indicating when the skipper should be called. The Mate can be left to his own devices with no more detailed instruction than 'have a quiet watch'. If possible, the most experienced watchkeepers should stand duty at the most difficult times, as when crossing shipping lanes.

As the skipper you must make it very plain to your watchkeepers exactly what they can and cannot do without consulting you, and a Night Order Book is most useful for this. In the back you list the standing orders for when to call the skipper; while in the front you give the specific instructions for individual watchkeepers each day.

THE WATCHKEEPER'S JOB

The essential task of a watchkeeper is to watch: the movement of other shipping that might give rise to a close encounter; the course steered by his own boat to ensure it is that ordered by the skipper; the weather for any sign of change and deterioration; the chart for the proximity of dangers; the sails and rigging for correct trim, chafe or breakdown; the engine, if running, and attendant gauges for signs of trouble; the bilges for signs of leaks; and other people for signs of seasickness, tiredness and lack of concentration.

As well as keeping watch the watchkeeper must also enter up the deck log hourly with all the information required by the skipper. This usually entails noting the wind speed and direction, sea state, barometer reading, course

NIGHT ORDERS : FRIDAY 16 MAY

__Sarah 2100-2359__

- steer to windward and note course averaged

- call me on sighting shipping lane ahead, or at 2300 if not sighted by then

__John 2359-0300__

- get shipping forecast 0033

- should raise loom of St John's light (Fl 3.15 sec) 30° on st'bd bow about 0145. Call me if not sighted by 0215, or if not on expected bearing

__George 0300-0600__

- call me 0530 with tea please

- expect rough water over Gannet Bank approx 0330-0430

- take soundings from 0300 and note times of crossing and leaving the bank

⌂ *A page from a skipper's night-order book.*

steered, estimated leeway, course alterations and so on. If the engine is running, the readings from all gauges should also be noted, although this is better done in a separate engine logbook, which can also contain details of maintenance.

Only the most highly experienced watch-keepers should be allowed the responsibility of taking avoiding action if another vessel is on a collision course, because it can be a much more complicated business than it often seems. The action to be taken may depend on many more factors than are visible to the watch-keeper, such as other ships over the horizon, nearby shoals or dangers. But determining whether risk of collision exists can be delegated to suitably competent watchkeepers, as long as they call you in good time if the slightest doubt exists. The ability to recognise the lights and shapes displayed by other vessels is essential to a watchkeeper, as it can save a lot of calls to the skipper to identify low-flying submarines and the like.

KEEPING A LOOKOUT

This is a vitally important part of watchkeeping and should be approached in a thoroughly professional manner. The basic technique is to sweep slowly round the whole horizon, from right ahead to right astern, with your eyes; then do the same with binoculars. Pause to relax your eyes for a few minutes then repeat the whole process. If you think you caught a glimpse of something but cannot see it when you look hard, then look slightly to one side of where you think it is. The retina in your eye is more sensitive to faint light at its edge, something that only shows up at times such as these, particularly when searching for distant lights at night. Be careful not to let white light into your eyes at night as it will blind you momentarily. More insidiously, it will reduce your visual efficiency for up to 20 minutes.

In fog you must also look with your ears. The sound of a ship's engine can be heard much further under water than through the air, so try going below now and then and listening with your ear pressed to the hull underwater. It will be very difficult to gauge the direction, but this will at least give some advance warning and an indication of whether the sound is approaching you or moving away. Post lookouts in the bows so as to see that bit further, and also to listen away from noise in the cockpit or the engine. In radiation fog try climbing the mast, as this type of fog is often very low-lying and you may see other masts over the top of it.

WATCHKEEPING SYSTEMS

Two watches
Night: 3 hours on
       3 hours off

Day: 6 hours on
       6 hours off

Three watches
    3 hours on
    6 hours off

Four watches
     3 hours standby
     (domestic & maintenance)
     3 hours on
     6 hours off

WATCHKEEPING ROUTINES

In principle each watch should be as long as possible consistent with the watchkeeper being able to stay alert (or awake!). This gives those off watch the maximum time for sleep. A reasonably experienced watchkeeper should be able to sustain six-hour daylight watches in fair weather, and three hours at night when it is more difficult to stay awake. A two-man crew working watch and watch about like this should be able to sail forever without succumbing to exhaustion. In bad weather or fog you should reduce these times to three daylight hours and two at night.

Whatever system you work – and there is no need to stick rigidly to the same one at all times – there are certain routines that should be adhered to. The new watch should be called 15 minutes before they are due to take over, which gives them time to dress, get their brains into gear, collect their night vision and turn up five minutes before the hour. They can then acclimatise to the conditions and have a proper handover.

This handover is important. The off-going watchkeeper should ensure that the relieving one is given all information about shipping, recent weather forecasts or changes, current skipper's instructions, sails set, the boat's position on the chart, any visible land or sea marks, the course being steered and so on. He should then check that the deck log is up to date before disappearing below.

SURVIVING A WATCH

A three-hour night watch in wet, cold and windy weather can be very wearing indeed, but there are certain techniques you can use to make it more bearable, not just for the comfort of the watchkeepers as such, but because the more miserable someone is the less efficient he is.

Proper sea-going clothing that will keep you warm and dry is obviously important, but simply sitting still in it for long periods reduces both its efficiency and your own. Foul-weather gear does not create heat, it simply helps to retain the heat which you generate. If you sit crouched and miserable in the corner of the cockpit, your body will not make heat for the clothing to keep in. Creeping lethargy brings on a mental depression and a slowing of the bloodstream, which then generate tiredness and coldness, so it is important to move about frequently, stamping your feet and swinging your arms to send the blood hurtling hotly through your veins. Under the oilskins you will find that many thin layers make for more effective insulation than a few thick ones, since they create a multitude of air pockets.

↪ *Keep moving, keep warm and stay happy.*

COURSE ORDERED (°C)	LOG READING	ESTIMATED			WIND	SEA	WEATHER	Vis	Bar	POSITION
		COURSE STEERED	DIST RUN	LEEWAY						
160	94.9	163	7.1	nil	W4/5	mod	2/8 H	G	17½	53° 26.2N : 01° 26.1E
,"	102.1	162	7.2							53° 23.5N : 01° 29.2E
	109.1	162	7.0						18	53° 20.8N : 01° 32.0E
	116.0	163	6.9		W4					53° 17.2N : 01° 34.8E
	122.9	162	6.9							53° 14.8N : 01° 37.5E
	129.3	160	6.4							53° 11.8N : 01° 39.9E
	135.5	160	6.2						18½	53° 09.4N : 01° 43.0E
	140	161	4.5		W3	slight	1/8 H			53° 08.1N : 01° 44.8E
	144.2	160	4.2							53° 06.2N : 01° 46.4E

⌂ Make sure the crew keep the deck log up to date throughout the night watch; you need that information to work up your DR plot.

You can boost your morale considerably by talking, brewing up, pottering about trimming sails or repairing things. If there are two of you on watch and conditions are reasonable then you can beneficially take turns to sit below in the warm for ten minutes.

STEERING ON WATCH

If there is more than one person in the watch the steering should be overseen by the watchkeeper. Half-hour tricks are usually long enough, particularly at night or in bad weather, since staring at a compass is very tiring under such conditions. It is much better to steer on a landmark or star and glance at the compass now and then to ensure that the course is correct. Bear in mind, however, that stars move and that tidal streams can cause landmarks to, in effect, do the same.

The watchkeeper must also check to see what course is actually being averaged, as opposed to the one ordered. This helmsman's error is quite normal and acceptable, but it is most important that it is noted for the benefit of the navigator. Different helmsmen will have different errors and this must be watched for. The deck log should have separate columns for the course ordered and course averaged, as well as estimated leeway. With all this information regularly assessed, the navigator will be able to run a much more accurate DR plot.

14 Heavy weather

Many sailors go for years without ever encountering seriously bad weather, but a skipper who does more than day-sailing must always be prepared for it. Although 'bad weather' immediately suggests strong winds and big seas, you should appreciate that poor visibility can, in many circumstances, be a great deal more dangerous than any strength of wind.

Wind in itself is, in truth, rarely the culprit when boats get into trouble. It is the waves: not the size of them so much as their shape; and it is important to understand that dangerous waves can be generated by quite moderate winds. Most often of all, however, the real culprit is the skipper.

THE SKIPPER'S ATTITUDE

Rough weather places extraordinary stresses on boat and crew, which can rapidly turn minor problems into major disasters. A sheet that does not lead perfectly fair, for example, may go quite unnoticed in moderate weather, yet prove impossible to harden properly in a gale when you desperately need that final ounce of efficiency for beating off a lee shore. A twisted tackle may be tolerated for months of calm summer weather, then cause a man to overbalance and crack his skull when the first real gale comes along. In heavy weather it is not enough for the gear to be in excellent condition; it must work perfectly too.

With everything working at top efficiency you should be able to approach heavy weather as though it is simply another point of sailing, much as a competent dinghy sailor views a capsize. This is a positive approach that will communicate itself to the crew, and they will smile and face the storm instead of cowering in the cockpit. The improvement in morale and efficiency that this generates can mean the difference between calmly getting home on time and not getting home at all. You must not be afraid of rough weather.

Fog, however, is something a skipper should always be afraid of, for the simple reason that it exposes his boat to the crass stupidity and incompetence of others. A good skipper may revel in the challenge of rough weather, but one who does the same with fog is a fool.

◊ *Well reefed down and under control.*

PREPARING THE BOAT

You should make your preparations for coping with heavy weather in plenty of time before the weather comes, as they are then so much easier to carry out. All loose gear should be securely stowed, deck gear firmly lashed down and hatches and scuttles shut and carefully secured. Reef the mainsail while the weather is still moderate, and either reef or change the headsails. Ensure that all halyards are sweated up tight and make a routine check of standing rigging bottlescrews, shackles etc. Check the tightness and security of the guardrails and jackstays.

Make a routine check of the engine, and top up the oil and fuel as necessary. If need be, run it for a while to charge the batteries right up, in readiness for the possible use of navigation lights, spreader lights and searchlights, navigation equipment and so on. Pump the bilges dry and switch off any automatic bilge pumps so that you can keep track of the ingress of any water. Check that all the bilge pumps are operating. Give at least half a dozen extra dry strokes to clear out any gas that might be in the bilges. A small and normally harmless amount may get shaken up sufficiently in rough seas to become dangerous.

The crew should be fed and the galley cleared up, dishes washed and put away and all domestic gear securely stowed. Prepare some heavy weather food in readiness – soup, sandwiches or whatever, depending on the size of boat and crew. When all this is done sit at your chart table and pre-plan as much of the next stage of navigation as you can, to save having to do it in the rough weather. Plot your expected course ahead; make detailed notes in the navigator's notebook of what you expect to see or pass, and also of any havens you think you might possibly have to run for. Check the course ahead for any potential dangers that the gale might cause – shallow banks, tidal overfalls and so on – and shape your course to pass well clear.

↻ *When the wind gets up you need to think about all the potential hazards that lie ahead.*

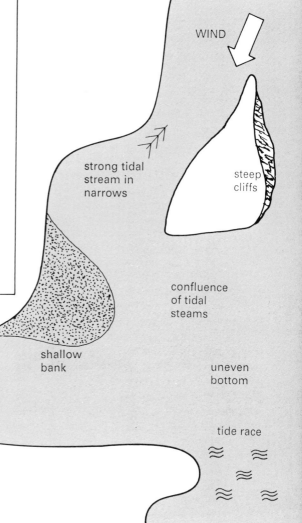

WIND

strong tidal stream in narrows

steep cliffs

confluence of tidal steams

shallow bank

river bar

uneven bottom

tide race

Many of these checks and preparations may seem trivial, but I cannot stress too much the confidence and control it gives you in bad weather to know that everything is totally secure and fully operational. This is what gives you the psychological edge over the weather and enables you to calmly dominate it and prevent it from doing the same to you. I never think of bad weather without seeing in my mind a photograph of an old Lowestoft sailing trawler with a truly monstrous wave towering over it. Sat on the weather bulwark, seemingly without a care in the world, are two old fishermen in smocks and sou'westers, puffing on their pipes. Clearly everything on that ship is absolutely secure and under control, and that is how it should be in that sort of weather.

PREPARING THE CREW

This is no less important than preparing the boat. A well-found crew in good spirits stands a much better chance of calmly handling bad weather than a tired and despondent one. The man in the club bar who boasts of staying awake wet and cold for 48 hours is simply advertising his incompetence. On a well-run boat people just do not stay awake wet and cold for 48 hours, or even a tenth of that time.

A competent skipper should be able to foresee the onset of bad weather in more than enough time to ensure that all his crew are rested, warm, dry and well-fed in readiness. Those prone to seasickness can often be given medication in sufficient time for it to take effect. Harnesses should be given out to the crew, who should try them on and fit them properly over their oilskins. Each crewman should then retain that harness all the time for his own use only. This ensures that he has one that fits, and when he needs it in a hurry he can simply put it straight on without having to fiddle about adjusting it: a small but important precaution that can save much time and frayed tempers when things get difficult.

You should organise your watch system so as to ensure maximum rest for each crewman and minimum time spent on the tiring task of steering. If someone is not required on watch, make him rest below so that he will be fit and ready when he is required. Organise the boat so that

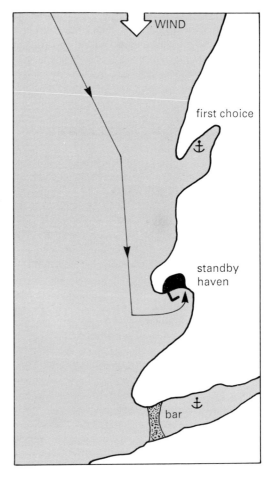

▷ Check the chart for downwind havens – you may need to run for one of them.

▷ Remember that some harbours may be dangerous to enter in an onshore wind.

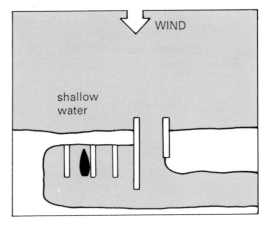

wet clothes and oilskins can dry out between watches, and make sure everything is clean and tidy down below to avoid the depressing effect of squalor. Above all, stay cheerful – for this will encourage calm and confidence in your crew.

HANDLING HEAVY WEATHER

A racing boat will clearly keep driving hard as long as it is safe to do so, but there is rarely any need to subject a cruising boat and her crew to this. If there is a risk of getting close to a lee shore during the expected duration of the gale then you should make all speed *beforehand* to get a good offing before it comes, in case you have to slow right down or heave-to when the gale is at its height.

The two safest places for riding out bad weather are the deep open sea and the pub. It is the bits in between these that get people into trouble. In wide-open deep water a competent crew should be able to handle most types of gear failure and so on with little more than moderate discomfort. With the shore or other dangers close to leeward even a minor problem can spell disaster.

Running for shelter is a very tempting course of action that is fraught with perils; it almost always gets you into worse trouble than ever you were in to begin with. Besides the risk of bad navigation or gear failure driving you ashore, there is the danger of being damaged or even overwhelmed by seas breaking in shallow water and strong inshore tides.

Big following seas make steering difficult, so make an effort to concentrate the sail area for'ard so as to pull the boat as straight as possible. Inexperienced helmsmen should be stood down in such conditions as they may allow the boat to broach, with possible serious consequences.

For more hints on dealing with bad weather, read *Heavy Weather Cruising* by Tom Cunliffe, also published by Fernhurst Books.

Dealing with fog
The pub is also a good place in which to ride out fog, but deep water certainly is not. The danger of collision with large ships steaming at full speed, totally reliant on radar sets that may

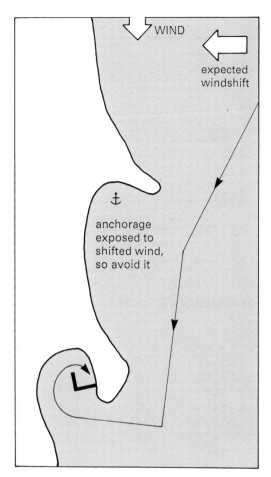

⌂ *If the wind changes, a safe haven could easily turn into a deathtrap in a gale. Make sure you are aware of any likely windshifts, and take account of them when you make your plans.*

be badly adjusted or badly operated, is far too great. In my view it is almost never justifiable for a pleasure yacht to put to sea in fog or with fog forecast, but if you do get caught out then the place to be is close inshore in water that is as shallow as navigational safety permits. This will enable you to keep close tabs on your position and it will also reduce considerably both the number and the size of vessels that can collide with you. If it seems prudent you can simply anchor and await the lifting of the fog, or you may be able to creep along with echo-sounder or leadline into a nearby safe haven. Note the points made in Part One about the different types of fog.

15 An offshore cruise

Now let us put all this into practice and see how we go about making a proper and successful offshore cruise, by which I mean one that is enjoyable and trouble-free. Rather than dream up an imaginary cruise, let me briefly recount a real one I made some years ago that does illustrate rather well some of the more important aspects of skippering.

I was working for the Island Cruising Club in Devon at the time, skippering a lovely old wooden ketch called *Irina VII*. The Club was a sort of cooperative, sailing a number of boats co-owned by all the members. Some of us were paid a little beer money to skipper cruises with other members on board, and this week three of our vessels set out on a cruise to the Channel Islands. *Irina* was joined by the old Brixham Trawler *Provident* (recently rebuilt and sailing again) and the big, sleek gaff schooner *Hoshi*.

A large anticyclone sat over the country as we set sail from Salcombe that Sunday afternoon and the three ships headed slowly towards the River Dart, working to windward in a light easterly breeze that barely ruffled the water in Start Bay. The passage to Dartmouth was no more than fifteen miles; a waste, some might say, of a whole precious afternoon out of the six days available for this cruise. The more experienced members on board knew better.

The Club had learnt, over its many years of running cruises in all kinds of vessels manned by all sorts of crew, that members who spent their working days in offices, classrooms and courtrooms were not acclimatised to the environment of a small sailing boat. However tough, however experienced, they all benefitted tremendously from a gentle introduction to a cruise: sleep aboard Saturday night, emergency drills and sail drill Sunday morning, then a short passage along the coast in the afternoon. A second night aboard and all would be fit for a crack-of-dawn start on Monday, ready to face anything. To embark on a dash out across a hundred miles of English Channel immediately after a long train journey, perhaps six months since last setting foot on a boat, would tax the best of them; the less tough could very easily have their whole week ruined.

By 0500 Monday, as the three ships ghosted quietly out of Dartmouth, all the crews were thoroughly acquainted with one another and their boats, all the skippers fully aware of everyone's abilities and characters, and all parties were raring to go. The weather pattern had been carefully studied by the three skippers all through the previous week's cruise and they were in a position to make a very accurate assessment of the likely conditions during the week. The drifting anticyclone seemed set to give an increasing breeze later that night, and the less weatherly gaffers, *Provident* and *Hoshi*, were none too confident

◊ Irina VII *going well to windward, despite a missing jib hank and a slack luff!*

about battering their way to Alderney, our destination. The consensus, however, was to give it a go and sail in company for the day.

Sailing in company with others can be great fun, and instructive; it can also be disastrous and unseamanlike in the extreme, especially with boats and crews of such varied abilities as we had. The danger, inevitably, is of having your decisions influenced unduly by those of the other skippers: 'George is going, so I reckon I should'. No skipper worthy of the name should ever think like this, however much he may respect George's ability and judgement, for the simple reason that the precise details of George's situation can never be exactly the same as yours. In this particular situation the very disparity of the boats made it relatively easy to ignore the decisions of the other skippers; if you sail in company with similar modern yachts, you will need to make a far more conscious effort to do the same.

Around midnight the freshening wind persuaded first *Provident* and then *Hoshi* to abandon the passage and return to England. *Irina* was a powerful 53-foot bermudan ketch from the stable of designer Alfred Mylne and builder

William Fife, and possessed far greater windward ability than the others, so, with a capable crew aboard, I felt perfectly confident about continuing towards Alderney.

We took in a couple of reefs and changed down to a smaller jib as the two other boats turned to show their sternlights. The sea was becoming lumpy and uncomfortable, as it does in the English Channel with an east wind, and we were in no great rush, being on time for a breakfast arrival off Braye Harbour on the northern tip of Alderney. I had been studying the weather forecasts, the shifting wind and the barometer all day and had by this time decided that we probably would not go in. The harbour is open to the north and this wind was quite likely to drift further north during the next day. At a steady force six it was much too strong to risk being caught in Braye if it went north.

We watched the entrance for a little while as we ate our breakfast, just so we could say we had been there, then tacked and ran back to the Ortac Channel just east of the Casquets, before squaring away for a storming reach down to Sark. The tide was running hard to the north-east at that time, against the strong wind,

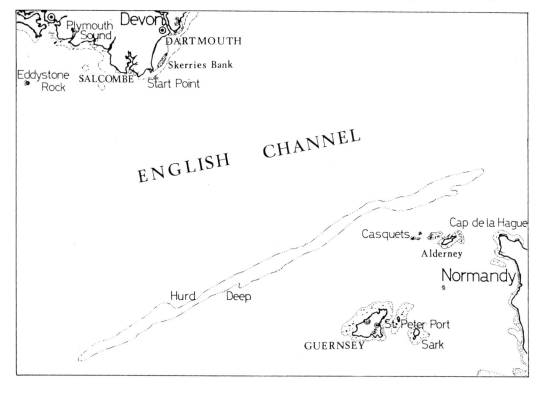

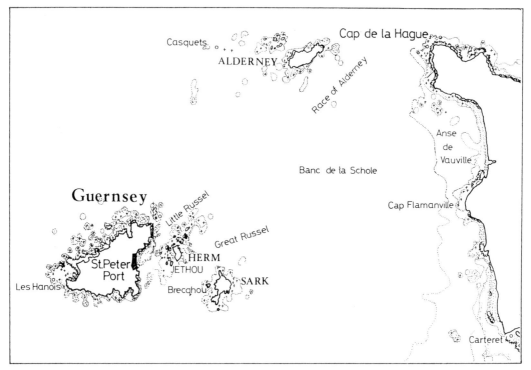

and neither the Alderney Race nor the Swinge channel appealed over-much in such conditions.

The Ortac would give us gentler seas in which to enjoy the broad reach and the sunshine – which we did. This small, but thoughtful decision made all the difference between a nerve-racking struggle and a glorious sail, and we were, after all, cruising. A skipper can make an awful lot of little decisions like this to change a difficult or arduous slog into pleasurable sailing. The capacity for so doing is the hallmark of a good cruising skipper; he is the one who has no dramas to report on arrival in harbour, just a crew who are all smiles and a boat in perfect condition.

Havre Gosselin, a delightfully snug and beautiful anchorage on the west side of Sark was our next and obvious destination in this wind, and it did not take us long to get there. There was, however, no need to race. We had all day to cover those few miles, so there was no temptation, as there often is, to crack on more sail when going downwind than we could safely set when on the wind. You should always bear in mind the possibility of having to suddenly round up onto the wind, for a man

overboard perhaps, or a navigational misjudgement – and set your downwind sails accordingly. There is considerable satisfaction and pleasure to be had from rolling downwind in a relaxed and controlled manner, knowing that should anything happen you have only to put the tiller down and haul in the sheets for everything to be perfectly under control. This is the essence, the satisfaction, and ultimately the real pleasure of cruising.

Havre Gosselin is totally sheltered from east winds but is normally approached from the south-west, as it lies just below Brecqhou. There is, however, a narrow passage between Sark and Brecqhou, through which you can approach Havre Gosselin direct from the north. The tide runs through it very hard, and we arrived as it was running against us. The passage is overhung by high cliffs and it was clear that we would run out of wind when we got inside, so I ran up the engine well beforehand to ensure that it was warmed through and tested before we committed ourselves to the entry, as the passage is far too narrow to anchor and swing in an emergency.

The other point that we had to consider here was the speed at which we would suddenly arrive in the anchorage as we came free of the tidal pull. Everything had to be prepared for rapid action: anchor and cable ready to run; halyards cleared away for lowering, and so on. The anchorage is small anyway, and if we came out of the passage to find it crowded we would have to act quickly. As it happened, the wind, having predictably fallen flat in the passage, suddenly blasted down the cliffs of Sark as we came into the bay and rounded up for the run in to anchor. Careful preparation, as ever, paid off.

A good night's sleep prepared us for another early start as we set out to 'do' all the Channel Islands in our week. Herm, Guernsey and Jersey lay ahead that Wednesday morning, and we would have to set off back to Salcombe some time Thursday evening.

The anticyclone had settled well over us by this time and little wind attended our drift down to Herm, where there is a rather exposed anchorage rarely suitable for a boat such as *Irina* to visit. It would have been a shame to waste the opportunity presented to us by this weather, and we were determined not to do so. Herm is about five miles from our anchorage at Sark but we contentedly spent all morning getting there, sunbathing, trailing a mackerel line and generally soaking up the atmosphere engendered by cruising around a delightful archipelago.

We spent the afternoon investigating the pink shell beach, the tiny island's own stamps and the pub that never closes, then set off under power to wind our way round a short-cut through the rocks in the gathering gloom of dusk, heading for St Peter Port in Guernsey. This gruelling two-and-a-half mile passage gave us a night on the town, a meal ashore, and left us with just Jersey to visit before sailing home late the next day. These two voyages – Sark to Herm and Herm to Guernsey – may not have inspired the 'thrash to windward' brigade, but they both added to the memories of this cruise.

At 0500 the next morning we headed slowly down the Little Russell under a shatteringly blue sky towards Grosnez Point on northern Jersey. We spent the afternoon alongside in the tiny fishing harbour of Bonne Nuit, thanks to local knowledge from a fisherman I knew, partook of his fresh crab for our supper, then finished off with a glorious night passage back to Salcombe, picking up our mooring late on Friday afternoon.

This was a marvellous cruise, one that I still remember after many years, partly due to the excellent weather but mainly because we packed so much variety into the week, assisted by the obvious benefits of cruising in an island group. Careful judging of the weather enabled us to cover a lot of ground, while still ensuring that we would make it home on time. May most of your cruises be just as good.

⊳ Irina VII *moored alongside the quay in Bonne Nuit, a tiny fishing harbour on Jersey.*

⊳ *End of a hard passage, and a well-earned alfresco meal in the cockpit.*

Appendix: Emergencies

MAN OVERBOARD

This is a very emotive subject on which vast amounts have been written, and it is all too easy, while wading through the many different techniques and costing out the gadgets, to completely lose all sense of proportion and rational judgement. The truth is that very, very few skippers ever lose a man overboard in circumstances requiring more than a line thrown to drag him alongside a boarding ladder. This latter piece of equipment may in rough conditions at sea pose the dangers that cause many writers to condemn it out of hand, but in most situations it will be found more useful than everything else put together. Make sure it fastens simply and securely to the boat amidships (where motion and freeboard are least and a lee can be made in rough weather) and ensure the bottom rung reaches far enough below the surface so that a man in the water can get a foot on it without having to reach upwards. A conscious man with one foot on the ladder like this is as good as rescued.

▷ It's almost impossible to heave someone back aboard over the guardrails, so cut them at the lashing. They are easy enough to re-rig.

The business of returning to someone who has fallen overboard at sea and been left behind poses a number of problems, the most important of which is undoubtedly the difficulty of seeing him. A dan buoy with an automatic

▷ Method 1: Flatten the guardrails and rig two lines: one to tie to the man and one to form a footloop.

Once his foot is in the loop he can climb aboard while the crew pull on his safety line. The loop can be raised to help him.

One last heave to get a knee on deck and the casualty is safely aboard again.

flashing light attached to a lifebelt is a good, simple solution to this, but it must be capable of guaranteed instant release by the helmsman without forcing him to leave his post. He can then concentrate fully on the next part of the process: getting the boat back to the man in the water.

There are two quite separate approaches to this, depending on circumstances. One is to manoeuvre immediately so as to remain close to the casualty and the other is to maintain an accurate course and speed until the boat can safely be turned and sailed back. With a competent helmsman and an easily-controlled boat there is much to be said for the former, while the latter action is probably safest for the inexperienced helmsman or an unmanoeuvrable boat (such as one with a spinnaker set or boom preventer rigged). As the skipper you must decide which action is to be taken and inform the watchkeepers accordingly.

Having returned to the casualty (see pages 43 and 48) your first action must be to get a line round him and secure him to the boat. What you then do will depend, as ever, on the situation, and there are a number of methods suggested for getting him aboard. Before getting involved in anything complicated, however, do bear in mind the necessity for speed to reduce the risk of the boat damaging him or hypothermia incapacitating him.

The quickest and simplest method is to grab the man by the arms and drag him straight over the gunwhale. With the guardrails lowered and the man on the lee side this is not as difficult as many proclaim. As a young fisherman I was taught how to use the waves and the rolling of the boat to heave aboard extremely heavy crab pots, and the same principle is taught for pulling men into liferafts. The basic idea is to heave when the gunwhale rolls down into a wave, thus bringing the man close to deck level. If necessary you then hold him there until the next wave gives sufficient lift to get him over the edge and onto the deck. In calm weather you should bounce the man up and down in the water a few times to build up momentum from his buoyancy, then give a final full-strength heave. Try this in a swimming pool; you will be surprised how effective it is.

There is no simple method for retrieving a man overboard in all circumstances and it is essential to appreciate that however much you may practise an apparently straightforward manoeuvre the real thing is likely to be somewhat different. It is vital that the system you adopt for your boat takes into consideration the type of boat and her gear, the possible difficulties created by complex rigs, and the abilities of all the crew who are likely to be left on watch as someone – and it might be you – goes over the side.

⇨ If the victim cannot help, drag him alongside and heave him partly clear of the water.

Push him back down, pull him up, push him down again and his own buoyancy will propel him upwards right out of the water.

Grab him as he comes up, haul him up onto the deck and help him recover. He may need first aid.

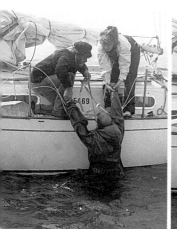

△ A third method involves using a spare halyard clipped to the casualty's harness.

While the crew holds on to the casualty's safety line to steady him the skipper starts to winch him up out of the water.

When his waist is level with the toerail the crew can grab him and heave him inboard.

FIRE

The technical skills involved in fighting a fire are not difficult, and it is very often the firefighter's attitude that determines whether he is successful or not. Speed and determination are absolutely vital since it is hard to believe, if you have not seen it, how quickly a small fire can turn into a raging inferno.

The basic secret is to corner a fire and work inwards with the extinguisher all round the edges, steadily reducing it in size. If you just blast the extinguisher into the middle the fire will go everywhere. Make sure the firefighter is kept supplied with extinguishers as a few seconds' delay after one runs out could enable the fire to roar out of control.

Do not be afraid to use water; even on fuel fires it can be employed safely if done so with care and understanding. Splashed over the *backs* of bulkheads and doors that are on fire it can cool them considerably and help prevent the fire spreading. This 'boundary cooling' is very important and should be continued for some while after a fire has gone out; it will remove residual heat which could erupt into another fire some hours later.

RIGGING FAILURE

The first essential, whether the mast goes overboard or not, is to prevent the situation

from deteriorating. Even the smallest rigging problem can escalate so rapidly into utter disaster that you must concentrate on preventing this rather than fixing the problem itself. If a 'ping' announces the disintegration of a shackle pin somewhere in the rig you must put about immediately to take the extra strain off the rest of the rigging. If you spot a missing split ring from a clevis pin, do not wander off to look for a new one; grab hold of the pin and hold it in place while sending someone else for a new one. And so on.

If the mast does go over, the first priority must be to stop it damaging the hull. Lash it very firmly alongside, haul it aboard or let it run clear on the end of a long warp to act as a sea anchor, depending on conditions. Do not let it bounce about alongside while you think how to get it back; get it clear or secure first.

HULL DAMAGE

There is an old saying that you should only ever step up into a liferaft (as the boat sinks under you). The implication is clear: you must have a very good reason indeed for abandoning an expensive, efficient and comfortable boat for a dangerous, wet and uncomfortable rubber dinghy. The ingress of water, in itself, is not sufficient reason; there are a thousand and one ways of getting it out and keeping it out and if you do suffer serious hull damage you should

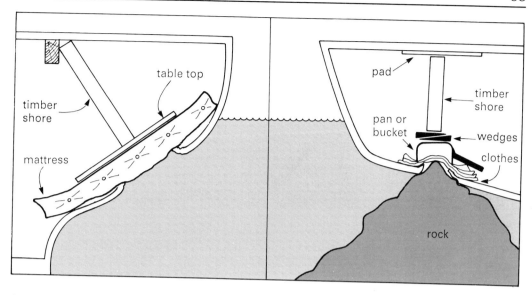

timber
shore

table top

mattress

pad

timber
shore

pan or
bucket

wedges

clothes

rock

be far too busy devising some to spend time abandoning ship or sending radio distress messages.

MECHANICAL BREAKDOWN

Contrary to much popular opinion these days this should not be an emergency for a sailing yacht. With proper maintenance it should not happen. It if does happen you should be able to fix it. If you cannot fix it you should be able to manage without it.

LOSS OF THE SKIPPER

Very rarely do skippers seem to consider the possibility that anything might happen to them. As a consequence most emergency procedures require the skipper's presence to carry them out efficiently.

This is fine, but at the same time you should be prepared for the worst, and produce some simple routines that will get the yacht and her crew to safety should anything happen to you. If you are lucky enough to have a competent Mate then he should be trained and briefed to fulfil this role alone. With a family crew, it is likely that all members may have to play their parts in dealing with this situation, and it will be necessary for you to work out these roles carefully, and brief the crew accordingly.

⌂ *Some ideas for keeping the water out.*

A single partner, insufficiently experienced to be left alone in charge of the boat, should nevertheless be taught sufficient to at the very least heave-to and call for help, using VHF radio and/or flares. It should be a relatively simple matter, particularly on a modern yacht, to teach almost anyone to heave-to, take the position from an electronic navigator, then make a Pan-Pan call on the radio. Hand flares can then be used as final identification of the yacht, on arrival of assistance. Even without electronic navigation aids, a well-kept logbook should provide a recent, timed fix or EP that can be transmitted; with no radio, parachute flares should be used according to a carefully-prepared pattern that will maximise chances of discovery.

Some thought needs to be put into these routines as it is essential they are simple enough for the person concerned to cope with under strain and possibly in a panic. How, for example, would your inexperienced partner get the spinnaker down alone and the boat hove-to in a breeze of wind if you fell overboard? What would he do if you had a heart attack while entering a busy or difficult harbour? How would he cope with a dismasting if you were incapacitated? This may sound far-fetched but an hour or two working out and practising a few simple routines could one day save both your lives.

Other yachting titles from Fernhurst Books

Cruising Crew *Malcolm McKeag*
Racing Crew *Malcolm McKeag*
Racing Skipper *Robin Aisher*
Tuning Yachts and Small Keelboats *Lawrie Smith*
Inshore Navigation *Tom Cunliffe*
Coastal and Offshore Navigation *Tom Cunliffe*
Celestial Navigation *Tom Cunliffe*
Simple Electronic Navigation *Mik Chinery*
Navigation at Speed *Tim Bartlett*
Heavy Weather Cruising *Tom Cunliffe*
Weather at Sea *David Houghton*
A Small Boat Guide to the Rules of the Road *John Mellor*
A Small Boat Guide to Radar *Tim Bartlett*
Electronics Afloat *Tim Bartlett*
Marine VHF Operation *J. Michael Gale*
Marine SSB Operation *J. Michael Gale*
Boat Engines *Dick Hewitt*
Motor Boating *Alex McMullen*
Children Afloat *Pippa Driscoll*
The Beaufort Scale Cookbook *June Raper*
On Passage *Mike Peyton*
Pasy: The Adventures of an Old Gaffer *John Jefferson*
Logbook for Cruising under Sail
The Motorboat & Yachting Logbook for Cruising under Power
Knots and Splices *Jeff Toghill*

Plus many more titles covering dinghy sailing, windsurfing, canoeing
and waterskiing

*If you would like a brochure giving information about existing and
forthcoming books, please send your name and address to:*

Fernhurst Books, 33 Grand Parade, Brighton,
East Sussex BN2 2QA, UK.

Or telephone: 0273 623174